INVISIBLE
DOCTRINE

INVISIBLE DOCTRINE

THE SECRET HISTORY
OF NEOLIBERALISM

**GEORGE MONBIOT
& PETER HUTCHISON**

CROWN
NEW YORK

A Crown Trade Paperback Original

Copyright © 2024 by George Monbiot and Peter Hutchison

Published in the United States by Crown, an imprint of the Crown Publishing Group, a division of Penguin Random House LLC, New York.
crownpublishing.com

CROWN and the Crown colophon are registered trademarks of Penguin Random House LLC.

First published in the United Kingdom by Allen Lane, an imprint of Penguin Press, in 2024. Penguin Press is part of the Penguin Random House group of companies.

Library of Congress Cataloging-in-Publication Data

Names: Monbiot, George, 1963– author. | Hutchison, Peter (Peter D.), author.
Title: Invisible doctrine : the secret history of neoliberalism / George Monbiot and Peter Hutchison. Description: New York : Crown, 2024. | Includes bibliographical references and index.
Identifiers: LCCN 2023058128 (print) | LCCN 2023058129 (ebook) | ISBN 9780593735152 (trade paperback) | ISBN 9780593735169 (ebook)
Subjects: LCSH: Neoliberalism—History. | Global environmental change—Economic aspects. | Climatic changes—Economic aspects. | Poverty. | Fascism.
Classification: LCC HB95 .M626 2024 (print) | LCC HB95 (ebook) | DDC 320.51/3—dc23/eng/20240131
LC record available at https://lccn.loc.gov/2023058128
LC ebook record available at https://lccn.loc.gov/2023058129

ISBN 978-0-593-73515-2
Ebook ISBN 978-0-593-73516-9

Printed in the United States of America on acid-free paper

9 8 7 6 5 4 3 2 1

Book design by Aubrey Khan

TO THE PROTESTERS

who stand up again and again for people and planet,
however often they are knocked down.

We are governed, our minds are molded, our tastes formed, our ideas suggested, largely by men we have never heard of.

EDWARD BERNAYS,
Propaganda (1928)

CONTENTS

1.

THE ANONYMOUS IDEOLOGY

Imagine that the people of the Soviet Union had never heard of Communism. That's more or less where we find ourselves today. The dominant ideology of our times—which affects nearly every aspect of our lives—for most of us has no name. If you mention it, people are likely either to tune out or to respond with a bewildered shrug: "What do you mean? What's that?" Even those who have heard the word struggle to define it.

Its anonymity is both a *symptom* and a *cause* of its power. It has caused or contributed to most of the crises that now confront us: rising inequality; rampant child poverty; epidemic diseases of despair; off-shoring and the erosion of the tax base; the slow degradation of healthcare, education, and other public services; the crumbling of infrastructure; democratic backsliding; the 2008 financial crash; the rise of modern-day demagogues, such as Viktor Orbán, Narendra Modi, Donald Trump, Boris Johnson, and Jair Bolsonaro; our ecological crises and environmental disasters.

We respond to these predicaments as if they occur in isolation. Crisis after crisis unfolds, yet we fail to understand their common roots. We fail to recognize that all these disasters either arise from or are exacerbated by the same coherent ideology—an ideology that has, or at least *had*, a name.

Neoliberalism. Do you know what it is?

So pervasive has neoliberalism become that we no longer even recognize it as an ideology. We see it as a kind of "natural law," like Darwinian selection, thermodynamics, or even gravity—an immutable fact, a nonnegotiable reality. What greater power can there be than to operate namelessly?

But neoliberalism is neither inevitable nor immutable. On the contrary, it was conceived and fostered as a deliberate means of changing the nature of power.

2.

THE "FREE" MARKET

What is neoliberalism? It's an ideology whose central belief is that competition is the defining feature of humankind. It tells us we are greedy and selfish, but that greed and selfishness light the path to social improvement, generating the wealth that will eventually enrich us all.

It casts us as *consumers* rather than *citizens*. It seeks to persuade us that our well-being is best realized not through political choice, but through economic choice—specifically, buying and selling. It promises us that by buying and selling we can discover a natural, meritocratic hierarchy of winners and losers.

"The market," it contends, will—if left to its own devices—determine who deserves to succeed and who does not. The talented and hardworking will prevail, whereas the feckless, weak, and incompetent will fail. The wealth the winners generate will trickle down to enrich the rest.

Neoliberals argue that an active state seeking to change social outcomes through public spending and social programs rewards failure, fuels dependency, and subsidizes the losers. It creates an unenterprising society, run by bureaucrats, who stifle innovation and discourage risk-taking, to the impoverishment of us all. Any attempt to interfere with the market's allocation of rewards—to redistribute wealth and improve the condition of the poor through political action—impedes the emergence of the natural order, in which enterprise and creativity are rightly rewarded. At the same time, neoliberals contend that government intervention and bureaucratic control will inevitably lead to tyranny, as the state gains ever more power to decide how we should live.

The role of governments, neoliberals claim, should be to eliminate the obstacles that prevent the discovery of the natural hierarchy. They must cut taxes, shed regulation, privatize public services, curtail protest, diminish the power of trade unions, and eradicate collective bargaining. They must shrink the state and blunt political action. In doing so, they will liberate the market, freeing entrepreneurs to generate the wealth that will enhance the lives of all. Once the market has been released from political restraints, its benefits will be distributed to everyone by means of what the philosopher Adam Smith called the "invisible hand." The rich, he claimed:

> . . . are led by an invisible hand to make nearly the same distribution of the necessaries of life, which would have been made, had the earth been divided into equal portions among all its inhabitants, and thus without intending it, without knowing it, advance the interest of the society.[1]

It is fair to say that it hasn't quite worked out like this. Over the past forty years, during which neoliberalism has prevailed both ideologically and politically, wealth—far from trickling down—has increasingly become concentrated in the hands of those who already possessed it.[2] As the rich have grown richer, the poor have grown poorer, and extreme poverty and destitution now blight even the richest nations. And while the state might have deregulated finance and other commercial sectors, leaving their bosses free to behave as they wish, it has reasserted control over other citizens—intruding ever further into our lives as it stifles protest and restricts the scope of democracy.

Even on its own terms, as this book will show, neoliberalism has failed—and failed spectacularly. It has also inflicted devastating harm on both human society and the living planet, harm from which we're at risk of never recovering. In terms of the spread and reproduction of its worldview, however, it has been astonishingly successful.

Over the years, we have internalized and reproduced neoliberalism's creeds. The rich have allowed themselves to believe they've secured their wealth through their own enterprise and virtue—conveniently overlooking their advantages of birth, education, inheritance, race, and class. The poor likewise have internalized this doctrine and begun to blame themselves for their situation. They become defined, from within as well as without, as losers.

So never mind structural unemployment: if you don't have a job, it's because you're unenterprising. Never mind the impossible costs of rent: if your credit card is maxed out, it's because you're incompetent and irresponsible.

Never mind that your school has lost its playing field or you are living in a food desert: if your kid is fat, it's because you're a bad parent.

The blame for systemic failure is individuated. We absorb this philosophy until we become our own persecutors. Perhaps it's no coincidence that we've seen a rising epidemic[3] of self-harm and other forms of distress, of loneliness, alienation, and mental illness.

We are all neoliberals now.

3.

THE FAIRY TALE OF CAPITALISM

Neoliberalism is often described as "capitalism on steroids." It treats some of capitalism's most oppressive and destructive practices as a kind of holy writ that must be protected from challenge, and tears down the means by which they might be restrained. If we are to understand neoliberalism, we must first understand capitalism.

Throughout the media we see an unremitting, visceral defense of capitalism—but seldom an attempt to define it or to explain how it might differ from other economic systems. It's treated as another natural law, as if it were the inevitable result of human evolution and endeavor.

But, like neoliberalism, capitalism didn't spring organically from the ground. Listening to some of its defenders, you could be forgiven for thinking that they may not be aware of the origins of capitalism—or perhaps even comprehend what it is.

The standard definitions are along these lines:

Capitalism is an economic system in which private actors own and control property in accord with their interests, and, in response to the constraints of demand

and supply, set prices in free markets. The essential feature of capitalism is the motive to make a profit.

Such definitions, however, are insufficient. They fail to distinguish the peculiarities of capitalism from the simple business of buying and selling, which in various forms has prevailed for thousands of years. They also fail to mention the coercion and violence upon which capitalism depends. With this in mind, we'd like to offer a definition we feel is more specific and precise, although it will take some unpacking:

> Capitalism is an economic system founded on colonial looting. It operates on a constantly shifting and self-consuming frontier, on which both state and powerful private interests use their laws, backed by the threat of violence, to turn shared resources into exclusive property, and to transform natural wealth, labor, and money into commodities that can be accumulated.

Let's explore what this means.

While capitalism's origins are disputed, we believe there is a case for tracing them to the island of Madeira,[1] 320 miles off the west coast of north Africa. Madeira was first colonized by the Portuguese in the 1420s. It was a rare example of a genuinely uninhabited island. The Portuguese colonists treated it as *terra nullius*: a "blank slate." They soon began clearing it of the resource after which it was named: *madeira* is Portuguese for wood.

At first, forests on the island were felled to meet the need for timber—which had been all but exhausted in Portugal and was in high demand for shipbuilding—and to clear land for raising cattle and pigs. In other words, the original colonists simply extended the economy with which they were familiar. But after a few decades, they discovered a more lucrative use of Madeira's land and trees: producing sugar.

Until that point, economies had remained, at least in part, embedded in religious, ethical, and societal structures. Land, labor, and money tended to possess social meanings that extended beyond the value that could be extracted from them. In medieval Europe, for instance, feudal economies—while highly oppressive—were strongly connected to both the Church and a codified social system of mutual obligation between large landowners and their serfs or vassals.

On Madeira, as the geographer Jason Moore has shown,[2] a form of economic organization developed that was in some respects different from anything that had gone before. On this newly discovered island, the three crucial components of the economy—land, labor, and money—were detached from any wider cultural context and turned into commodities:[3] products whose meaning could be reduced to numbers in a ledger.

Onto the blank slate of Madeira's land, the colonists imported labor in the form of slaves, first from the Canary Islands 300 miles to the south and then from Africa. To finance their endeavors, colonists imported money from

Genoa and Flanders. Each of these components—land, labor, and money—had been stripped of their social meanings before. But arguably not all in the same place, at the same time.

By the 1470s, this tiny island became the world's biggest source of sugar. The fully commoditized system that the Portuguese created was astonishingly productive. Using slave labor, freed from all social constraints, the colonists were able to produce sugar more efficiently than anyone had done before. But something else was new—the amazing speed at which that productivity peaked and then collapsed.

Sugar production on the island peaked in 1506, just a few decades after it began. Then it fell precipitously, by 80 percent within twenty years—a remarkable rate of collapse. Why? Because Madeira ran out of *madeira*. Stoking the boilers needed to refine and process a kilogram of sugar required 60 kilograms of wood. The enslaved laborers had to travel farther and farther afield to find this wood, extracting it from ever steeper and more remote parts of the island. In other words, more labor was needed to produce the same amount of sugar. In economic terms, the productivity of labor collapsed, tumbling fourfold in twenty years. In tandem, the forest clearance drove several endemic Madeiran animal species to extinction. The island-wide disturbance of forest ecosystems was sufficiently serious that the first of several major extinctions of endemic mollusks occurred in the early sixteenth century, the result of "rapid and large-scale change in the habitat, from woodland to grassland."[4]

So what did the Portuguese sugar planters do? They did what capitalists everywhere would go on to do. They left. They took their operation to another recently discovered island farther south, São Tomé, 190 miles off the west coast of central Africa. There the pattern that had been established on Madeira was repeated: Boom, Bust, Quit.

When sugar production on São Tomé went bust, the Portuguese moved on again—this time to the coastal lands of Brazil, where their much bigger operations followed the same script: Boom, Bust, Quit. Then other imperial powers moved to the Caribbean, with the same results, burning through one frontier after another. Since then, the pattern has been followed across countless commodities and commercial schemes—the sparks that ignited Madeira's forests scattered across the world. They continue setting fire to ecosystems and social systems to this day, consuming all that lies in their path. This seizure, exhaustion, and abandonment of new geographical frontiers is central to the model we call capitalism.

"Boom, Bust, Quit" is what capitalism *does*. The ecological crises it causes, the social crises it causes, the productivity crises it causes are not perverse outcomes of the system. They *are* the system.

Before long, Portugal was supplanted by other nations, and England quickly became the dominant colonial power. Over the course of the next several centuries, European colonial powers systematically looted one region after another. They stole labor, land, resources, and money, which they then used to stoke their own industrial revolutions. The United Kingdom's great and unequal wealth was built on colonial theft in Ireland, the Americas, Africa, India, Australia, and elsewhere. One estimate suggests that, across two hundred years, Britain extracted from India alone an amount of wealth equivalent to $45 trillion in today's money.[5]

To handle the greatly increased scope and scale of transactions, the colonial nations established new financial systems that would eventually come to dominate their economies—instruments of extraction whose use has intensified. It continues today with ever-increasing sophistication, assisted by offshore banking networks.[6] Powerful people and corporations seize wealth from around the world and hide it from the governments that might otherwise have taxed it, and from the people they have robbed. As offshore tax havens and secrecy regimes shift capital ever further out of sight, this disappearing act has created its own new capitalist frontier in the invention of evermore creative financial schemes.

Using international debt and the harsh conditions attached to it (a system known as "structural adjustment"),[7] tax havens and secrecy regimes, transfer pricing (moving wealth between subsidiaries),[8] and other clever instruments, rich nations have continued to loot the poor, often with the help of corrupt officials and the proxy governments they install, support, and arm. Commodity traders working with kleptocrats and oligarchs fleece poorer nations—seizing their natural resources, effectively without payment. The US research group Global Financial Integrity estimates that $1.1 trillion a year flows illegally out of poorer nations,[9] stolen through tax evasion and the transfer of money within corporations.

If this rapacious cycle were interrupted, the system we call capitalism would fall apart. Capitalism depends upon constant growth, and must forever find new frontiers to colonize and exploit. So now its attention turns to the deep ocean floor, in search of mineral clusters to mine, and fish populations yet to be driven to exhaustion. It looks to outer space, seeking to extract minerals from planets and asteroids, or to stake out new colonies:[10] escape hatches for the super-wealthy to be exploited once Earth is no longer habitable.

A system based on perpetual growth cannot exist without peripheries and externalities (the "unintended," and often devastating, consequences of economic activity). There must always be an extraction zone, from which materials are taken without full payment; and a disposal zone, where costs are dumped in the form of waste and pollution. As the scale of economic activity increases, so capitalism transforms every corner of the planet—from the atmosphere to the deep ocean floor. The Earth itself becomes a sacrifice zone. And its people? We are transformed into both the consumers and the consumed.

All exploitative systems require justifying fairy tales, and the true nature of capitalism has been disguised from the beginning by such myths and fables. The Portuguese colonists on Madeira claimed that there had been a natural apocalypse,[11] a wildfire that raged for seven years, consuming all the wood on the island. There was an apocalypse all right, but there was nothing natural about it. The island's forest was incinerated by a different blaze—the fires of capitalism.

The fairy tale of capitalism grew wings in 1689, when John Locke published his *Second Treatise of Civil Government*.[12] Locke claimed that "in the beginning all the world was America." By this, he meant a *terra nullius*: like Madeira, a no-man's-land in which wealth was just waiting to be taken. But, unlike Madeira, the Americas were heavily inhabited—by tens of millions of indigenous people. To create his *terra nullius* they would have to be erased—either eradicated or enslaved.[13]

But this was just the beginning of Locke's mythmaking. He went on to claim that the right to own land, and all the wealth that sprang from it, was established through hard work. When a man has "mixed his labour" with the land, Locke asserted, he "thereby makes it his property."

Of course, indigenous peoples around the globe had spent thousands of years mixing their labor with the land, long before European colonists arrived. But Locke, without ever acknowledging that he had done so, created a Year Zero, a unique and arbitrary moment at which a particular person—a European man of property, of course—could step onto a piece of land, stick a spade into the earth, and claim it as his own. After he had "mixed his labour" with the land at this fairy-tale moment, a colonist could erase all prior rights and claim all future rights, as soon as the metal made contact with the soil. He and his descendants thenceforth acquired exclusive and perpetual rights to the land—the land they had stolen—and the right to do with it as they chose.

"But hang on . . . ," you may ask, "did European men of property actually drive that spade into the ground with their *own* hands?" This question exposes another of capitalism's justifying myths: that one person's labor can belong to another. As was often the case with colonial enterprise, it wasn't the men of property who were breaking a sweat; rather, it was the labor they claimed to own. While scholars still debate Locke's contradictory views on slavery, his claim that after a man has "mixed his labour" with the land, then he "thereby makes it his property," validated the acquisition of large-scale property rights via slave ownership.

When you strip capitalism's justifying myths away, you see something that should be obvious. Capitalism is not, as its defenders insist, a system designed to distribute wealth, but one designed to capture and concentrate it. The fairy tale that capitalism tells about itself—that you become rich through hard work and enterprise—is the greatest propaganda coup in human history.

4.

RISE OF THE NEOLIBERAL INTERNATIONAL

Neoliberalism—the explosive accelerant of capitalism—also has a history. A history of which few people are aware.

The term "neoliberal" was coined at a conference in Paris in 1938.[1] Among the delegates were two of the people who came to define the ideology: Ludwig von Mises and Friedrich Hayek. Both exiles from Nazi-occupied Austria, they saw the New Deal that Franklin Roosevelt had introduced in the United States, and Britain's burgeoning welfare state, as expressions of collectivism. They believed that any form of collectivism—putting the interests of society before the individual—would lead inexorably to the kind of totalitarianism that had swept across Europe, in the form of Nazism and Communism.

In 1944, Friedrich Hayek published his best-known book, *The Road to Serfdom*,[2] in which he explained this theory. He argued that the welfare state—and social democracy in general—would, through reducing the scope of individual action, eventually mutate into the sort of absolute control exercised by Stalin and Hitler. Ludwig von Mises's book, *Bureaucracy*[3]—published the same year—

made a similar argument. Both books were widely read, and they became especially popular among very wealthy and powerful people. These people saw in Hayek's and von Mises's ideas an opportunity: an opportunity to escape from the tax, regulation, and labor movements against which they and their fortunes chafed. They quickly began to take an active interest and to bankroll the spread of this new ideology.

The Road to Serfdom found a particularly receptive audience among business conservatives in the United States. Not only did it appear to justify the political changes they wanted to see, but it also redefined their financial self-interest as a courageous stand against tyranny and a principled defense of freedom. They set out to ensure that as many people as possible were exposed to Hayek's arguments.

DeWitt Wallace, the anti-communist cofounder (with his wife) and editor of *Reader's Digest*—with eight million subscribers the most popular magazine in the United States at the time—published a condensed version of *The Road to Serfdom*.[4] One million reprints were ordered, many of them by companies keen to indoctrinate their employees. The book gained even greater circulation when *Look* magazine published a cartoon version,[5] which, among other corporate outlets, was distributed by General Motors to its workers. In 1945, Hayek traveled to America for a speaking tour, and was received, for example, by 3,000 people at New York's Town Hall.[6, 7] Supported by serious money, this old-fashioned Viennese academic became a sensation, touring the United States and speaking at local chambers of commerce and bankers' associations.

In 1947, Hayek formed the first organization to promote neoliberalism, the Mont Pelerin Society (MPS).[8] There, he and others began to create what has been described as a "Neoliberal International"[9]—a transatlantic network of academics, journalists, and businesspeople seeking to develop a new way of seeing and running the world.

Over the next twenty years, as the doctrine spread, the money poured in. Hayek's network was financed by some of the world's richest people and businesses,[10] including DuPont, General Electric, the Coors Brewing Company, the wholesale drug giant William Volker & Co., Charles Koch (Koch Industries), Richard Mellon Scaife (banking, oil, aluminum, and newspaper magnate), Lawrence Fertig (advertising executive and libertarian journalist), and the steel magnate William H. Donner.

The rich backers hired policy analysts, economists, academics, legal experts, and public-relations specialists to create a series of "think tanks" that would refine and promote the doctrine. These institutions, many of which still operate today, tended to disguise their purposes with grand and respectable names, such as the Cato Institute, the Heritage Foundation, the American Enterprise Institute, the Institute of Economic Affairs, the Center for Policy Studies, and the Adam Smith Institute. While they presented themselves as independent bodies offering dispassionate opinions on public affairs, in reality they behaved more like corporate lobbyists, working on behalf of their funders.

The same rich backers also underwrote academic departments in universities, such as the University of Chicago[11, 12] and the University of Virginia.[13, 14] Again, these departments presented themselves as independent and objective, but the main effect of their work was to propagate and amplify the ideology. The University of Chicago in particular, thanks to this generous patronage, established itself as a laboratory for the extension of neoliberal ideas, and remains a crucible of the doctrine to this day. The William Volker Fund—a small but influential conservative foundation that, by the late 1940s, was spending about $1 million a year on neoliberal advocacy projects—helped underwrite Hayek's salary at the University of Chicago for over a decade.[15] The fund gave the same support to von Mises at New York University.[16]

Employing cutting-edge methods of persuasion in the burgeoning fields of modern psychology and public relations to brilliant effect, these highly skilled thinkers and strategists began creating the language and arguments that would transform Hayek's anthem to the elite into a viable political program. Their efforts at spreading the doctrine more broadly were highly creative: Hayek's arguments were repackaged as serialized cartoons;[17] while the beloved children's books of Laura Ingalls Wilder were rebranded as a celebration of self-sufficiency, limited government, and economic and individual freedom.[18, 19, 20]

As it evolved, neoliberalism became more strident. For example, Hayek initially opposed monopoly power. But in 1960 he published another best-selling book, *The Constitution of Liberty*,[21] in which he radically changed some of his arguments. The book marked the transition from an honest if extreme philosophy to a sophisticated con. By then, the network of lobbyists and thinkers that Hayek had founded was being lavishly funded by multimillionaires, who saw the doctrine as a means of liberating themselves from political restraints on their freedom of action. But not every aspect of the neoliberal program advanced their interests. With *The Constitution of Liberty*, Hayek appears to have adjusted his position to meet their demands.

He began the book by advancing the narrowest possible conception of liberty: *an absence of coercion*. Hayek rejected the primacy of such notions as democratic freedom and equality, universal human rights, or the fair distribution of wealth, all of which, by restricting the behavior of the rich and powerful, intruded on the absolute freedom from coercion—that is, the freedom to do whatever you want—that neoliberalism demanded. Democracy, by contrast, he claimed, "is not an ultimate or absolute value." In fact, Hayek argued, liberty depended upon preventing the majority from exercising choice over the direction that politics and society might take. (This position echoes James Madison's concerns about how the "excessive democratic power" of the masses could lead to the oppression of the "minority rights" of the elite).[22, 23]

Hayek justified this position by creating a heroic narrative of extreme wealth. He conflated the economic elite—spending their money in new and creative ways—with philosophical and scientific pioneers. Just as the political philosopher should be free to think the unthinkable, so the very rich should be free to do the undoable, without constraint from public interest or public opinion. The ultra-rich are "scouts," "experimenting with new styles of living," who blaze the trails that the rest of society will follow.

The progress of society, Hayek held, depends on the liberty of these "independents" to gain as much money as they want, and to spend it as they wish. All that is good and useful therefore arises from inequality. A free society, in his mind, became one in which the state helped eliminate firebreaks that prevented capitalism's conflagration from consuming the world. It may come as no surprise to those who follow such matters that in 1974 Hayek was awarded the Nobel Prize for Economics.

Something else happened at around the same time: the movement lost its name. Until 1951, for example, economist Milton Friedman—perhaps Hayek's most famous disciple—was happy to call himself a neoliberal.[24] But soon afterward, the term more or less disappeared from the literature that he and others published. Stranger still, no alternative appeared with which to replace it.

At first, for all the lavish spending, neoliberalism remained at the political margins. There was a fairly solid international consensus built around John Maynard Keynes's prescriptions: governments should pursue full employment; taxes should be high and public services well funded; inequality should be constrained and a social safety net should prevent the poor from falling into destitution. Despite the success of Hayek's books, the neoliberal program of empowering the rich and letting the devil take the hindmost was met with widespread public revulsion.

It wasn't until the 1970s, as the postwar economic boom finally came to an end and Keynesian economics began to run into various crises, that neoliberalism was able to occupy the resultant ideological vacuum. The success of Keynes's model relied to a large extent on capital controls,[25] fixed exchange rates, and strongly regulated financial markets, which both prevented speculators from sucking money out of national economies and ensured that government stimulus measures (cutting interest rates or increasing spending on public services) catalyzed manufacturing and jobs at home rather than in other countries with competing industries. When, in 1971, Richard Nixon abandoned the system of fixed exchange rates, he opened the door for speculation and capital flight.[26] These were among the factors, in combination with the Middle East oil crisis of 1973, which led to a disastrous combination of high inflation, high unemployment, and a decline in productivity growth.

These were not simply numbers on an economist's balance sheet. New York City, as one striking example, was forced to declare bankruptcy in 1975:[27, 28] by then it was already notorious for urban decay and all that comes with it—crime, drugs, poverty, and empty city lots. This created a great deal of fear and anxiety—something neoliberals saw as opportunity. As Milton Friedman said, after three decades of development, "When the time came, we were ready . . . and we could step straight in."[29]

With the help of sympathetic government advisers and journalists, neoliberal ideas—especially regarding monetary policy—began to seep into the administrations of Jimmy Carter in the United States and James Callaghan in the United Kingdom.[30] Hayek was said to be Ronald Reagan's favorite political philosopher;[31, 32, 33] Milton Friedman would become Reagan's close adviser while he was in office.

In 1975, a few months after Margaret Thatcher became leader of the Conservative Party, one of her colleagues (or so the legend goes) was explaining what he saw as the core beliefs of conservatism. She snapped open her handbag, pulled out a dog-eared book, and slammed it on the table.[34] "This is what we believe!" she said. The book was *The Constitution of Liberty*.

Like Reagan, Thatcher surrounded herself with advisers who sought to transform Hayek's ideas into a political platform, combining neoliberal economics with a revival of nineteenth-century social conservatism: tradition, family, and the veneration of work.

At the time, people referred to these political programs as "Thatcherism" or "Reaganism." But these weren't ideologies in their own right; they were merely applications of neoliberalism. Their massive tax cuts for the rich, the crushing of trade unions, the reductions in public housing, deregulation, privatization, and the outsourcing of public services were all proposed by Hayek or his disciples. The ideology that had been incubated for three decades in think tanks and academic departments—with the generous support of wealthy backers—had hatched.

As these governments began to implement their programs, the Neoliberal International machine set out to ensure they were popularized. The most effective of its advocates was Milton Friedman. He understood the rhetorical power of simplicity and possessed a talent for turning

Hayek's complex ideas around privatization, deregulation, and individual freedom into accessible and catchy concepts.

Friedman famously used the common pencil as a way of illustrating the "invisible hand" in economics:[35] the pencil's constituent parts (American wood, South American graphite, Malaysian rubber, and so on) were brought together by "the magic of the price system," which, he argued, not only resulted in "productive efficiency," but, incredibly, "foster[ed] harmony and peace among the peoples of the world." His book *Capitalism and Freedom* would go on to sell half a million copies, and in 1976 he, too, received the Nobel Prize for Economics. In the 1980s, PBS gave Friedman his own TV series—*Free to Choose*—a sprawling ten-part infomercial for neoliberalism beamed into households across the United States. Friedman's masterstroke was implanting the idea that "business freedom *is* personal freedom" in the minds of Americans.

A political revolution that would sweep the world had begun.

5.

THE NEOLIBERAL ERA

The real triumph of the Neoliberal International network was not its capture of the right, but its subsequent colonization of the parties that once stood for everything Hayek detested.

The Democratic and Labor Party leaders who followed in Reagan's and Thatcher's wake did not possess a meaningful alternative to the neoliberal narrative. Rather than developing a new political story, Bill Clinton and Tony Blair thought it was sufficient to *triangulate*. In other words, they extracted a few elements of the Keynesianism their parties had once advocated, mixed them with aspects of their opponents' neoliberalism, and developed from this unlikely combination a "Third Way."

This "Third Way" was little more than a rhetorical device used to justify and disguise the capitulation of the left to neoliberal forces. Nowhere has this been clearer than in the United States. For all Clinton's talk of being a "new Democrat," he adopted the core principles of neoliberalism. As well as pushing through the George H. W. Bush administration's unfinished work on global trade agreements, Clinton signed legislation that would further deregulate the financial and telecoms industries, disempower organized labor, and hollow out the welfare state.[1, 2] When Clinton pronounced that "the era of big government is over,"[3] what he meant was: "neoliberalism rules supreme."

In hindsight, it seems inevitable that the blazing, insurrectionary confidence of neoliberalism would exert a stronger gravitational pull than the dying star of social democracy. Hayek's triumph could be witnessed everywhere, from Blair's expansion of the Private Finance Initiative in 1997 (that led to the privatized management of everything from schools to hospitals to prisons) to Clinton's repeal of the 1933 Glass-Steagall Act (that had been pushed through Congress by FDR's administration to regulate the financial sector in the wake of the Great Depression).

For all his grace and touch, Barack Obama (who didn't possess a narrative either, except for "hope") was guided by neoliberalism's vast apparatus—by then dominating the perspectives of both government and the media, its doctrines treated as orthodoxy across the political spectrum. Upon entering the White House in 2009, in the turbulent aftermath of the financial crash of 2007–2008—and with the help of a campaign financed by some of America's wealthiest plutocrats[4, 5, 6, 7, 8]—Obama had the opportunity to break from neoliberalism's cage, to confront the powers that "the market" disguised and the social divisions it caused. But he chose not to take it. He bailed out the banks, but failed to impose the kind of penalties that would discourage bankers from repeating their lucrative mistakes.[9] He proposed new trade treaties that would give corporate lobbyists and neoliberal ideologues everything they wanted: reducing environmental and labor standards and curtailing state sovereignty. Grace and decency alone cannot defeat structural injustice.

As neoliberalism became the norm—as governments, left and right, gradually withdrew from governance and left crucial social and economic issues in the hands of an abstraction called "the market"; as the very rich, released from the taxes and rules that once restrained them, captured ever more of the wealth generated by society; as the choice between different parties, committed to the same program to varying degrees, increasingly narrowed—people began to lose faith in politics. Disappointment turned to disempowerment. Disempowerment turned to disenfranchisement.

Public services were allowed to founder. Large numbers of people saw their wages flatline and their pensions shrink. The financial sector, released from regulation, almost tanked the global economy. The authors of this disaster escaped unpunished. As a result of these failures, politics came to seem less and less relevant to people's lives. Political debate sounded like the empty rhetoric of a remote elite. Some of the disenfranchised turned instead to a virulent anti-politics, in which facts and arguments are replaced by slogans, symbols, and sensation.

The man who sank Hillary Clinton's bid for the presidency in 2016 was not Donald Trump. It was her husband.

6.

WHAT'S LIBERAL ABOUT NEOLIBERALISM?

It may seem strange that a doctrine promising choice and freedom should have been promoted by Margaret Thatcher with the slogan "There is no alternative." But when Friedrich Hayek visited General Pinochet's Chile in 1981, he told a journalist that he preferred a "liberal dictator" to "a democratic government devoid of liberalism."[1] (By "liberalism" he meant neoliberalism, but by then he would no longer speak its name.)

So what did freedom, in this case, mean? Freedom from trade unions and collective bargaining means freedom for bosses to suppress wages. Freedom from regulation means the freedom to exploit and endanger workers, to poison rivers, to adulterate food, to design exotic financial instruments, to charge exorbitant rates of interest. It leads to train wrecks—both literally and figuratively—from the recent string of toxic spill derailments in the American Midwest,[2, 3, 4] to the financial meltdowns and bank bailouts we now seem to have accepted as an inevitable fact of economic life. Freedom from taxation—which, by definition, involves the redistribution of wealth—throttles a crucial mechanism to help lift the poor out of poverty. The "freedom" that neoliberals celebrate—which sounds so beguiling when expressed in general terms—turns out to be freedom for the pike, not for the minnows.[5]

Hayek believed, or claimed to believe, that "the market" would automatically protect society from tyranny and serfdom. But the "market forces" he so revered had to be administered—as capitalism had been from the outset—and enforced by the state.

Cultural critic Stephen Metcalf points out that "this is what makes neoliberalism 'neo.'"[6] He argues that previous doctrines, such as "classical liberalism" or "laissez-faire economics," had promoted, like neoliberalism, a "free" market and a minimal state. Merchants from the seventeenth century onward had demanded that governments leave them alone—to *laissez-nous faire*. But neoliberalism developed in a different era, by which point most adults had the vote. It recognized that, in the face of widespread resistance, the state would have to intervene to impose its desired political outcomes on an unwilling population, to liberate "the market" from democracy.

As Naomi Klein showed in her book *The Shock Doctrine*,[7] neoliberalism has often been imposed on people during great crises: at moments when they were too distracted to resist—or even notice—the new policies that governments were slipping under their doors. It was introduced, for instance, by force in the aftermath of Pinochet's 1973 coup in Chile. It was intensified in the wake of the American invasion of Iraq in 2003, when the US administration captured and privatized the country's assets. It was employed in 2005, in the aftermath of Hurricane Katrina in New Orleans. As the disaster unfolded, resulting in thousands of fatalities and vast environmental destruction, Milton Friedman remarked, "Most New Orleans schools are in ruins, as are the homes of the children who have attended them. The children are now scattered all over the country. This is a tragedy. It is also an opportunity to radically reform the educational system."[8]

Augusto Pinochet's coup in Chile is widely seen as inaugurating the global neoliberal era. As the 1970s progressed, neoliberal ideas and policies came increasingly to shape the agendas of international financial institutions, including the World Bank and International Monetary Fund, which imposed neoliberal economics on indebted nations in Africa, Latin America, and Asia.[9] In return for debt relief or loans, "structural adjustment programs" were demanded, which included privatization, deregulation, trade liberalization, the abandonment of capital controls, and "fiscal austerity," which meant slashing state spending on health, education, and other public services. These decisions were imposed without people being given the chance to vote on them: the poorer nations had no choice but to implement them, regardless of what their populations thought.

In other words, when neoliberal policies couldn't be imposed domestically, they were imposed internationally. Unwilling nations also found themselves subject to the whims of big business, as offshore courts[10]—presided over by corporate lawyers—sprung up around the world, allowing corporations to sue states if they didn't like the legislation passed by their parliament or congress. For example, a government or parliament might announce that oil companies will be forbidden from drilling in inshore waters. Or that cigarette firms will no longer be allowed to advertise their wares. Or that pharmaceutical corporations may no longer charge absurd prices for the drugs they sell to the health service. Regardless of the fact that these decisions were made by elected representatives, the offshore arbitration system known as Investor State Dispute Settlement (ISDS) allows those "aggrieved" corporations to sue the nation. If the nation loses, their democratic decisions are overturned—so much for national sovereignty. Corporations often emerge with more sovereign power than states.

According to the United Nations Conference on Trade and Development (UNCTAD), the total ISDS case count had reached more than 1,100 by the end of 2020, affecting 124 countries.[11] In several cases, corporations are suing governments for introducing climate policies that "diminish the value of investments."[12] In separate cases, the German energy companies RWE and Uniper have brought claims against the Netherlands, alleging that its proposed phaseout of coal power plants was a violation of the Energy Charter Treaty.[13] The Canadian company TC Energy recently initiated a NAFTA "legacy claim," seeking $15 billion in damages from the US government as a result of its decision to cancel the Keystone XL pipeline project.[14, 15]

The majority of claims are brought by companies based in rich nations,[16] and are often imposed upon far weaker countries that have fewer resources with which to defend themselves. The ISDS has become little more than a form of colonial looting by other means.

It is highly misleading to describe neoliberalism as "free-market economics." In many ways it's quite the opposite. Neoliberalism is the tool used by the very rich to accumulate more wealth and power. Neoliberalism is class war.

7.

"RENT" AND OTHER AMBIGUITIES

While the doctrine was not conceived as a self-serving racket, during the neoliberal era it rapidly became one. Beginning around 1980 in the United States and United Kingdom, rates of economic growth were much lower than the average during the Keynesian era[1]—but not for the very rich. Up to this point, inequality had declined for some sixty years. But from the 1980s onward, it returned with a vengeance.[2] Since 1989, America's super-rich have grown about $21 trillion richer.[3] The poorest 50 percent, by contrast, have become $900 billion poorer.[4]

Why? Because trade unions, essential for securing higher wages, were crushed. Because tax rates for the very rich were slashed. Because regulations that big business viewed as constricting were loosened or eliminated. And, perhaps most important, because *rents* were allowed to soar.

What is rent? The term has several meanings that are readily confused, so let's take a moment to clarify. In this context, rent means *unearned income*. It's the "private tax" that the owners of property or services can charge, above and beyond any investment they've made, to the people who wish to use them. Remember that capitalism, under our definition, "turns shared resources into exclusive property." Once this has happened, resources previously used by common agreement within a community come to belong to a single family or a single corporation. This entity can then charge others for the right to use them. For example, everyone needs land—land to live on, land to travel over, land to work on. But when land is captured and enclosed by one person, that person can charge the rest of the community for the right to use it.

Why is this basic fact of economic life so poorly understood? Partly because "rent" is one of many crucial economic terms whose meaning has been obscured. Rent is most commonly used to mean the money you pay to lease a home. But this single payment has two entirely different components. One is the compensation you pay to the owner for the services they provide to you: the bricks and mortar, the fixtures and fittings, the refurbishments they might have made. The other is the fee you must pay the owner for access to the crucial and nonreplicable resource on which the home stands—land. In many countries, the land is the greatest component of the cost of a home: in the UK, for example, 70 percent of the cost of housing arises from the price of the land on which the home is built.[5] Homes are more expensive in more desirable locations not because bricks and mortar cost more in such places, but because of the higher price of the land on which they stand. So when you pay "rent" for a home in the UK, 30 percent of that money, on average, provides you with the shelter you need. The rest is the charge you pay to use the space it occupies.

Importantly, this concept of rent is not confined to housing and real estate. Neoliberalism has enabled those it favors to convert an ever-wider range of shared resources into exclusive property, permitting the expansion of capitalism's frontier.

Public services, in the main, have been built through the common endeavor of entire societies. State schools, hospitals, social care, water systems, transport and energy networks, parks and other public lands, prisons, libraries, and municipal buildings were all created by states in response to public need or public demand, often backed by advocacy campaigns in which millions participated. These initiatives have been largely financed by public taxes, and built and staffed by public-sector workers, many of whom went above and beyond the call of duty both to create and to sustain the services in which they believed.

One of the fundamental "reforms" pursued by neoliberalism was to privatize these public services (or at least as many as capitalism's servants in government could get away with), transferring collective resources into exclusive ownership. We can still use them, but now, on top of the payment that the state or the customer makes for the actual service provided (water, or sanitation, or transport, or hospitals, or housing), we have to pay—either individually or as taxpayers—an extra fee to those whose exclusive property the service has become. This fee is what we mean by rent.

Think of it as a tollbooth. When public services are privatized, the new owners place a tollbooth in front of them through which we must pass. What we find on the other side may or may not meet our needs, but to get there we must pay the toll. Because this access fee is bundled with the price of the actual services we receive, it's difficult to disentangle the toll from the total cost. But the toll— the rent we must pay—is the reason for the disproportionate price of the water that comes through our pipes, the electricity that comes through our wires, and for healthcare in places like the US, where some of the world's most rapacious corporations have been allowed to charge outrageous fees. The owners of essential and life-giving services have us over a barrel.

Invariably, public services were sold (in some cases gifted) to private owners at far less than their real value. There are some grotesque examples: in India and Russia, for instance, ruthless and well-positioned opportunists grabbed or were granted, at moments of crisis, crucial assets through fire sales, creating a new and unimaginably rich class of oligarchs. In Mexico, a vast tranche of the nation's mobile-phone and landline services were handed to Carlos Slim, who soon became the world's richest man.[6] As a general rule, privatization is legalized theft from the public realm.

Roman Abramovich, once the owner of the Chelsea football club, offers a lurid example of how oligarchic power is built.[7] In a classic case of crisis-as-opportunity, he first became wealthy during the mayhem of Russia's rushed privatization in the 1990s, following the collapse of the Soviet Union. In the largest transfer of public assets to private owners in world history, an economy that once consisted almost entirely of state-controlled industries (manufacturing plants, oil refineries, mines, media outlets, biscuit factories, etc.) was suddenly privatized. Russia's most profitable industries were sold to predetermined recipients (i.e., friends of the Kremlin) at pennies on the dollar. Once the dust had settled, six Russian oligarchs, in one estimate, controlled half of Russia's economy.[8]

Abramovich's stake in the Russian oil company Sibneft (51 percent) cost him and his partner about $200 million in the mid-1990s. In 2005 he sold his stake back to the government for a reported $13.1 billion ($20.5 billion in today's money).[9]

Almost inevitably, privatization leads to a decline in both access to, and the quality of, public services. There's no mystery about why this should be: the owners' incentive is to extract as much money from the service as possible. They can do this in two ways: charge higher fees or cut corners, diverting money that should otherwise have been invested in improving the service into their own pockets. In privatized public services around the world we have repeatedly witnessed this legalized theft, as money previously used to improve schools, parks, or water-treatment works has instead been siphoned off as dividends.

Profitable components of public services are wrung dry, while essential but unprofitable aspects are dumped. People with complex health conditions are either abandoned or returned to the state for treatment, sewage treatment plants are bypassed and left to deteriorate,[10] bus services to smaller towns and communities are slashed. The ethos of public services shifts to reflect their new role as cash cows for capitalist enterprises. Hospitals are rebranded as "care businesses," universities become "knowledge businesses." Humanities and the liberal arts are denigrated, while governments emphasize (but still underfund) "economically useful" subjects: science, technology, engineering, math.[11] The result is widespread institutional failure, with services often driven to the brink of collapse.

We end up with what the economist John Kenneth Galbraith described as "private opulence and public squalor":[12] the rich become ever wealthier, while the services on which the rest depend are hollowed out.

Perhaps the most ubiquitous form of rent is "interest." Interest is the access fee charged for the use of another essential resource: money. The scope of this form of rent-seeking has greatly expanded under neoliberalism, through a process known as financialization: the intrusion of financial elites, institutions, and mechanisms into ever-wider aspects of our lives. For example, in many parts of the world, university students no longer receive state grants for their tuition. Instead, they're forced to rely on loans from the financial sector, accumulating significant debt. This debt, in turn, restricts their career options—in some cases forcing young adults to turn to the corporate world for higher salaries, instead of enhancing community life through teaching, counselling, not-for-profit work, and other forms of public service.[13] As the poor become poorer and the rich become richer, the rich acquire increasing control over money. This may seem obvious, but it still needs stating: interest payments flow primarily to the rich. They are another driver of inequality.

We're surrounded by such misleading or confusing terms. Take "investment." Business, government, and the media use this word to mean two entirely different things.[14] One is the use of money to create productive and socially useful assets or services that did not previously exist; the other is to capture and milk assets already in existence. A private-equity company might "invest" in housing without paying for a single brick to be laid upon another. What the word means in this context is buying existing buildings in order to charge rent or to benefit from their rising price.

By confusing *enterprise* with *rent*, the word "investment" disguises this extractive activity. It treats the construction of a toll barrier—through which people have no choice but to pass and surrender their hard-earned money—as a genuinely productive occupation.

Today, no one wants to be seen as a *rentier*: an economic parasite living off the work of others. As a result, a remarkable inversion has occurred. A century ago, entrepreneurs—people who had made their own money—were looked down upon by the "nobility" or "gentry" who had inherited their wealth and received their incomes from rent. "Old money" deployed a wide range of pejorative terms to denigrate new money, often borrowing French words—as the upper classes do when they discuss things that are too distasteful to describe in English—*nouveau riche, arriviste,* and *parvenu,* as well as the more direct *bounder* and *upstart.* They made haughty comments about people who "bought their own furniture."[15]

As a result, entrepreneurs seeking social acceptance tried to pass themselves off as aristocrats. They adopted the manners, style, and dress codes of the rentiers. Whenever possible, they married titled people and bought the stately homes that old money had vacated.

Now the situation has been flipped on its head: those who make their money from rent seek to pass themselves off as entrepreneurs. People like Donald Trump, who inherited their wealth and then used it to build businesses based on fleecing those who work for their living, insist that they're the authors of their own good fortune, having achieved economic dominance through hard work and enterprise.

Why has this reversal happened? Because neoliberalism does two contradictory things at once. It valorizes and fetishizes competitive enterprise, while in reality rewarding and empowering the established wealth that controls crucial assets, such as land. It has simultaneously created a strong social ethic of enterprise and a strong economic ethic of rent-seeking. By stripping away public protections and privatizing public services in the name of stimulating entrepreneurship, neoliberalism has created a bonanza for those who parasitize genuine enterprise. In other words, it consumes what it celebrates.

As we've witnessed, neoliberal policies are everywhere beset by market failure. It's not just the banks that are "too big to fail"; now it's also the corporations delivering public services. When society is reliant upon these corporations to deliver healthcare, water, transportation, or electricity, the free-market competition that neoliberals so revere is never allowed to run its course.[16] Even in the most debased democracies, public services can't be allowed to collapse completely, for fear of civil unrest. "Investors" must always be rescued by the state. This insulates them from risk. They can pursue strategies that will enrich them while destroying the services they are supposed to provide, knowing that if they go under, either the state will bail them out or they can walk away. Wealth is transferred from the poor to the rich, and the public is saddled with their debts.

8.

THE REDISTRIBUTION
OF WEALTH

There was a time when it seemed as if the lives of everyone in the richer nations would inexorably improve. Democracy and capitalism appeared, during this period, to be compatible. Everyone could expect to see their wealth, rights, and freedoms increase. From the Second World War until the late 1970s, general prosperity rose steadily.[1] The total income captured by the top 1 percent declined. The rising tide genuinely seemed to lift all boats.

There were two principal reasons for what seemed, at the time, to be unstoppable growth. The first is a familiar one: the rise of social democracy.

The destruction of the wealth and power of the elite, caused largely by two tectonic events—the Depression and the Second World War—created an opening for the redistributive policies of John Maynard Keynes, among others. A more equal distribution of wealth, accompanied by increased state spending and a strong social safety net, enhanced the spending power and economic security of those who had previously lived in poverty, boosting their demand for goods and services. This generated growth that further boosted demand in a cycle that seemed, during the "glory years" of 1945 to 1975, to be self-sustaining.

The second reason, far less discussed, is that the fruits of colonial and postcolonial looting were also more evenly apportioned.

The steady rise of prosperity across the Global North during this period was, to a large extent, financed by the Global South. We look back on the era when Keynesian economics dominated as a time of peace and prosperity, and many in the wealthier nations experienced it as such. But it was also a time in which decolonization was resisted with extreme violence and oppression by the colonial nations, and nascent independence was partially reversed through the coups and assassinations that these wealthy countries engineered or supported. Among these assaults on the peace and prosperity of other nations were the overthrow of Mohammad Mosaddegh in Iran in 1953, the crushing of Jacobo Árbenz's government in Guatemala in 1954, the murder of Patrice Lumumba in Congo in 1961, Suharto's coup in Indonesia in 1967, and Pinochet's violent overthrow of Salvador Allende in Chile in 1973.

The coup in Chile was the experiment upon which Margaret Thatcher and Ronald Reagan both drew when they came to power, respectively in 1979 and 1981. Pinochet's economic program was devised and overseen by neoliberal economists from the University of Chicago, and enthusiastically supported by Milton Friedman,[2] Friedrich Hayek, and the Neoliberal International. Released from the restraints of democracy, Pinochet's economists were able to implement the entire neoliberal package: Chileans who resisted were imprisoned, tortured, or murdered. The nation's resources were systematically plundered, especially its principal asset, its copper mines. Unrestrained by either democratic resistance or state regulation, American and European corporations were free to take what they wanted, often without payment. Redistributive taxes and progressive spending were terminated. Inequality skyrocketed.[3] The inevitable result was a series of extreme economic crises, from which Chile has yet to recover. As the rich grew richer, the poor worked harder.

The Global North's postimperial interventions were justified with the rhetoric of the Cold War—defending the Western sphere of influence against Soviet expansionism— but their underlying purpose was to secure resources and territory for the dominant capitalist powers. By dismantling the fireguards of independence and democracy— stripping entire populations of their political agency—such interventions ensured that capitalism's fire-front would continue to expand across the world.

In looking back on the Keynesian era, we have a tendency to see two seemingly contradictory histories—the march of social progress in the rich nations and the brutal wars, resource grabbing, and social regress in the Global South—and to discuss them as if they occurred on separate planets. But these apparently divergent trends are, in fact, closely connected. One of the distinguishing features of the Keynesian era is that a greater number of people in the Global North got to dip their fingers in the sack of stolen goods. At no point, however liberal its pretensions, has the fundamental condition of capitalism been altered: it is, and has always been, "an economic system founded on colonial looting."

In other words, during the "glory years," economic life within the rich nations was fairer than it had ever been before—or has ever been since. But relations between rich and poor nations during the Keynesian era remained grossly unjust and coercive. Neoliberalism's contribution was to ensure that economic life became grossly unjust and coercive *everywhere*—even within the richest of nations.

In the United States, for example, during the 1960s and early 1970s, the greatest beneficiaries of economic growth were the poorest 20 percent. But from 1980 onward, the proceeds of growth were transferred from the poorest people to the ultra-rich.[4] Median income in the US rose at just one-third of the rate of GDP growth, while the income of the richest 1 percent rose at three times that rate. By comparison to the pre-neoliberal trend, the bottom 90 percent lost $47 trillion between 1975 and 2018. Conversely, between 1990 and 2020 the wealth of US billionaires, adjusted for inflation, increased roughly twelvefold.[5]

There's a similar story in other nations. In the UK, wages have stagnated,[6] while the costs of living—especially housing—have soared. Since the beginning of the Covid-19 pandemic, the world's 10 richest men have doubled their wealth,[7] while an additional 163 million people have been pushed below the poverty line.[8]

Across the thirty-eight nations in the Organisation for Economic Co-operation and Development (OECD), which can be broadly characterized as the "rich world," taxation has taken a regressive turn: the rich pay less, while the poor pay more.[9]

The result, neoliberals claim, would be that economic efficiency and investment would rise, enriching everyone. But the opposite has occurred. As taxes on wealthy people and corporations diminished, the spending power of both the state and poorer people contracted, reducing economic demand.

Neoliberalism promised that it would generate growth and that the benefits of this growth would "trickle down" from the rich to the poor, enhancing everyone's conditions of life. But, as a wide range of academic studies and statistics show,[10] the connection between economic growth and general prosperity in rich nations broke down years ago.[11] For better or worse, growth has been slower globally during the neoliberal era than during the years before Thatcher, Reagan, and their many imitators came to power.[12] And this growth has, overwhelmingly, been captured by the very rich. Far from ensuring that money trickles down, neoliberalism is the hydraulic pump that drives the transfer of wealth from the poor to the rich.

During the "golden age" of social democracy, governments in the rich world treated growth as a means to an end, leading to higher standards of welfare and well-being for everyone. But neoliberalism treats growth as an end in itself, entirely divorced from utility, like the ruthless production targets of Mao Zedong in Communist China. To feed this insatiable beast, we must toil ever harder and destroy ever more of the world on which our lives depend. Previous generations of economists foresaw a time when so much wealth was generated that we would scarcely need to work.[13] Despite that level of wealth having been reached, we instead find ourselves working to the point of burnout.

Why? Because growth has been used by successive governments as a substitute for distribution. If we just keep working harder, "one day" we'll generate the public services we need; "one day" we'll earn the economic security we crave. But everywhere we're told "not yet," as "we can't afford it." This is a claim made endlessly by governments that go on to squander vast sums on civil and military white elephants, corporate welfare and bailouts, giveaways to favored interests, and tax breaks for the rich. Will this magic day ever arrive? Of course not—that's the point. Well-funded public services and economic security were never part of the plan—quite the opposite, in fact. But to have us working ever-longer hours on behalf of capital, as our lives become increasingly precarious? That is very much part of the plan.

Of course, growth under any system is of questionable benefit if its impact is to accelerate us toward Earth systems collapse. Perhaps it's time we recognized that "prosperity" has less to do with growth than with the distribution of power. When neoliberalism prevails, only the rich prosper. When democracy prevails, the prosperity of the poor, and of society as a whole, is enhanced. The general welfare of the nation depends, above all, on its position on that spectrum. None of the power shifts of neoliberalism are accidental. The doctrine is sold to us as a means of enhancing freedom and choice. In reality, it's about who dominates whom.

The way public money is spent has also changed. The economic anthropologist Jason Hickel points out that many countries with lower GDP per capita have longer life expectancies and better educational systems than the United States.[14] Why? Because, rather than allowing the rich to capture the great majority of economic growth, countries such as South Korea, Portugal, and Finland invest sensibly in public services. That's not to say they necessarily spend more. The crucial difference is that their investments are aimed at general prosperity rather than prosperity for a few. The United States spends four times as much on healthcare as Spain does—yet the lives of Americans, on average, are five years shorter.

A study of ten European nations found that changes in happiness could best be explained not by varying rates of economic growth, but by varying levels of spending on public welfare.[15] The high level of public investment and social support in Nordic countries—from universal healthcare, to free (or highly subsidized) quality education, to solid social safety nets—has contributed to overall well-being. Who would have guessed that economic security and strong public services could make us happier?

We talk of "the failure of the state," but the neoliberal state is broken by design. Its failures are engineered, grounded in an insistence that government cannot—and should not—solve our problems. It is not *supposed* to work.

After forty years of this experiment, it's become clear that the economic triumph neoliberalism proclaimed is illusory. Although the success of Keynesianism relied upon colonial looting, it generated economic growth, in part, by enhancing the spending power of those at the bottom. Neoliberalism, in contrast, has generated economic growth by pushing workers to the limit, accelerating resource extraction, and inflating asset values and household debt.[16] It is an incendiary device—burning through human relationships and the fabric of our planet, faster and more ruthlessly than Keynesianism did.

For while neoliberal capitalism continues to loot the South to enrich the North, it also loots the future to enrich the present.

9.

THE CRISIS OF DEMOCRACY

Perhaps the most dangerous aspect of neoliberalism is not its economic impact, but its political impact. As states become less willing to protect those at the bottom, to contest inequality and redistribute wealth, to provide effective public services, and to restrain those who seek to exploit us and the living planet, our ability to change our lives through voting diminishes. Neoliberals tell us we can vote with our wallets—that consumerism is its own democratic exercise and reward. But in the great "consumer democracy," some people have more voting power than others.

This leads us back to a term that, once again, disguises more than it reveals: "the market." What do you picture when you hear that word? Little stalls in public squares with striped awnings, selling cheese, or vegetables, or second-hand clothes, run by people of modest means? "The market" sounds like a friendly, egalitarian, democratic sphere. But, when used in the neoliberal context—"let the market decide"—the term disguises a host of power relations. "The market" becomes a euphemism for the power of money. When "the market" decides, it means that those who have the most power within the economic system—in other words, those with the most money—make the decisions. Political power is captured by economic power. Democracy is supplanted by plutocracy.

Perhaps the most concise definition of neoliberalism has been suggested by William Davies, a professor at Goldsmiths College in London. He calls it "the disenchantment of politics by economics."[1] It sucks the power out of people's votes.

Neoliberalism is a political neutron bomb. The outward structures of politics—such as elections and parliaments—remain standing, but following the irradiation of market forces, little political power remains to inhabit the space behind the facades. Real power shifts to other forums, inaccessible to ordinary citizens: quiet backroom meetings between government ministers and corporate lobbyists; fundraising dinners and holiday retreats; trade treaties and offshore tribunals; private meetings at economic summits. Because voters demand restraints on economic power—whether that involves restricting corporate concentration, the antisocial behavior of businesses and the very rich, extreme inequality, or environmental destruction—democracy is the problem that capital is always striving to solve. Neoliberalism is the means of solving it.

When the thick mesh of interactions that binds us to the state—cherished and effective public services, laws that protect the weak as well as the strong, a sense of shared civic life and citizenship, mutual obligation and fair exchange—are stripped away, all that remains are the worst aspects of state power: coercion and oppression.[2] The state becomes our enemy.

In the thirty years following the Second World War, there was a broad political consensus. Taxpayers and politicians alike recognized that the best defense against fascism was to ensure that everyone's needs were met through a strong social safety net and robust public services. But neoliberalism dismantled these defenses. Instead, it has promoted extreme self-interest and egocentricity. At its heart is a mathematically impossible promise: everyone can be number one.

In the gap between great expectations and low delivery, humiliation and resentment grow. History shows that when political choice is lacking and people see no prospect of relief, they become highly susceptible to the *transfer of blame*.[3] This transfer—attacking refugees and fomenting culture wars—is already well under way. Techniques of distraction—scapegoating, an intense focus on issues that have little impact on general welfare ("woke" academics, curatorial decisions in museums and historic houses,[4] unisex bathrooms, young people allegedly identifying as cats[5])—coupled with frustration and the transfer of blame, open the door to authoritarianism.

As neoliberalism erodes democratic choice; as it breaks up communities; as it destroys economic security; as it allows the rich to grab what they will; as political parties fail to offer an alternative, remedies, or hope, men like Trump, Johnson, Modi, Netanyahu, Putin, Orbán, Milei, Erdogan, Wilders, and Bolsonaro seize their chance. Such so-called strongmen—who claim to be advocates for the aggrieved and disenfranchised, armed with the promise of a return to traditional values—appeal to those who have been failed by the system. But once in power, they intensify the two main residual functions of the state: further empowering the rich and crushing dissent.

Individual demagogues come and go, but the broad trend is a worldwide shift toward authoritarian politics and a "democratic recession."[6] One study suggests that around 72 percent of the world's population now lives under "some form" of authoritarian rule.[7] The 2022 Freedom House report determined that only 20 percent of the world's population currently lives in fully "free" and democratic societies.[8, 9]

Unless democratic politics can be revitalized, this shift may have only just begun. The belief that the world was emerging permanently from the grip of tyranny, an idea promoted by the media's favored public intellectuals during the 1990s and 2000s, has proved ill-founded. On the contrary, democracy, confronted with untempered capitalism, is almost everywhere in retreat.[10]

Fascism emerges in situations where the state fails, where politics fails, where our needs can no longer be met through the democratic process. What Friedrich Hayek claimed to fear—the rise of a new totalitarianism—has been accelerated by his own doctrine.

10.

THE LONELINESS OF NEOLIBERALISM

Neoliberalism promotes not just the extreme individuation of responsibility, but also the extreme individuation of human life.

It assaults our mental health and drives deep into our social lives. It is perhaps no coincidence that the neoliberal era has been accompanied by epidemics of mental illness—including anxiety, stress, depression, social phobia, eating disorders, self-harm, and loneliness.[1] For the past decade, "deaths of despair" in the United States—suicides, overdoses, and alcohol-related illnesses—have been rising rapidly, particularly among middle-aged white men and women.[2, 3] In 2010, 20,000 people in the United States died by drug overdose; by 2021, that number had risen to more than 100,000.[4]

In 2021, life expectancy dropped by 2.7 years[5, 6]—the largest two-year decline since the First World War—of which Covid was but one factor among many.

There are plenty of secondary reasons for rising levels of distress, but there is also a plausible underlying and more fundamental cause: human beings, ultra-social mammals whose brains are wired to respond to other people, are being forced apart. Technological change plays a major role, but so does ideology. Although our well-being is inextricably linked to the lives of others, we're told at every turn to go it alone: that prosperity and public well-being are achieved through competitive self-interest and extreme individualism.

You can tell a lot about a society from its quirks of language. We repeatedly misuse the word "social." We talk about social distancing when we mean physical distancing. We talk about social security and the social safety net when we mean economic security and the economic safety net. While economic security comes (or should come) from government, social security arises from community. One of the extraordinary features of the response to Covid-19 is that, during lockdowns, some people—especially the elderly—received more community support than they had had in years,[7] as their neighbors checked up on them and offered to run errands.

Social media can help to fill the void, creating connections that did not exist before. But it can also intensify social comparison to the point at which, having consumed all else, we start to prey upon ourselves. Another ugly manifestation of the competition neoliberalism fetishizes is that it encourages us to quantify our social standing, comparing the number of online "friends" and followers we possess to other people's. Influencers feed us impossible aspirations, just as our real opportunities contract.

Neoliberal ideology has radically altered our working lives, leaving us isolated and exposed. The "freedom and independence" of the gig economy it celebrates, in which regular jobs are replaced by an illusion of self-employment, often translates into no job security, no unions, no health benefits, no overtime compensation, no safety net, and no sense of community.

In 1987, Margaret Thatcher said the following in a magazine interview:

> I think we have gone through a period when too many children and people have been given to understand "I have a problem, it is the Government's job to cope with it!" or "I have a problem, I will go and get a grant to cope with it!," "I am homeless, the Government must house me!" And so they are casting their problems on society, and who is society? There is no such thing! There are individual men and women and there are families, and no government can do anything except through people and people look to themselves first.[8]

As always, Thatcher was faithfully repeating the snake-oil remedies of neoliberalism. Precious few of the ideas attributed to her were her own. They were formulated by men like Hayek and Friedman, then spun by the think tanks and academic departments of the Neoliberal International. In this short quote, we see three of the ideology's core tenets distilled:

> First, everyone is responsible for their own destiny, and if you fall through the cracks, the fault is yours and yours alone.

Second, the state has no responsibility for those in economic distress, even those without a home.

Third, there is no legitimate form of social organization beyond the individual and the family.

There is genuine belief here. There is a long philosophical tradition, dating back to Thomas Hobbes,[9] which sees humankind as engaged in a war of "every man against every man." Hayek believed that this frantic competition delivered social benefits, generating the wealth that would eventually enrich us all. But there is also political calculation.

Together we are powerful, alone we are powerless. As individual consumers, we can do almost nothing to change social or environmental outcomes. But as citizens, combining effectively with others to form political movements, there is almost nothing we cannot do. Those who govern on behalf of the rich have an incentive to persuade us that we are alone in our struggle for survival and that any attempts to solve our problems collectively—through trade unions, protest movements, or even the mutual obligations of society—are illegitimate or even immoral. The strategy of political leaders such as Thatcher and Reagan was to atomize and rule.

Neoliberalism leads us to believe that relying on others is a sign of weakness, that we all are, or should be, "self-made" men and women. But even the briefest glance at social outcomes shows that this cannot possibly be true. If wealth were the inevitable result of hard work and enterprise, every woman in Africa would be a millionaire. The claims that the ultra-rich make for themselves—that they are possessed of unique intelligence or creativity or drive—are examples of the "self-attribution fallacy."[10] This means crediting yourself with outcomes for which you were not responsible. The same applies to the belief in personal failure that assails all too many at the bottom of the economic hierarchy today.

From birth, this system of belief has been drummed into our heads: by government propaganda, by the billionaire media, through our educational system, by the boastful claims of the oligarchs and entrepreneurs we're induced to worship. The doctrine has religious, quasi-Calvinist qualities: in the Kingdom of the Invisible Hand, the deserving and the undeserving are revealed through the grace bestowed upon them by the god of money. Any policy or protest that seeks to disrupt the formation of a "natural order" of rich and poor is an unwarranted stay upon the divine will of the market. In school we're taught to compete and are rewarded accordingly, yet our great social and environmental predicaments demand the opposite—the skill we most urgently need to learn is cooperation.

We are set apart, and we suffer for it. A series of scientific papers suggest that social pain is processed[11] by the same neural circuits as physical pain.[12] This might explain why, in many languages, it is hard to describe the impact of breaking social bonds without the terms we use to denote physical pain and injury: "I was stung by his words"; "It was a massive blow"; "I was cut to the quick"; "It broke my heart"; "I was mortified." In both humans and other social mammals, social contact reduces physical pain.[13] This is why we hug our children when they hurt themselves: affection is a powerful analgesic.[14] Opioids relieve both physical agony and the distress of separation. Perhaps this explains the link between social isolation and drug addiction.[15]

Experiments summarized in the journal *Physiology & Behavior*[16] suggest that, given a choice of physical pain or isolation, social mammals will choose the former. Children who experience emotional neglect, according to some findings,[17] suffer worse mental-health consequences than children suffering from both emotional neglect and physical abuse: horrible as it is, violence at least involves attention and contact. Self-harm is often used as an attempt to alleviate distress—another indication that physical pain can be more bearable than emotional pain. As the prison system knows only too well, one of the most effective forms of torture is solitary confinement.

It is not hard to determine what the evolutionary reasons for social pain might be. Survival among social mammals is greatly enhanced when they are strongly bonded with the rest of the group. It's the isolated and marginalized animals that are most likely to be picked off by predators or to starve. Just as physical pain protects us from physical injury, emotional pain protects us from social injury. It drives us to reconnect.

It is unsurprising that social isolation or loneliness has been strongly associated with depression,[18] suicide,[19] anxiety,[20] insomnia,[21] fear, and the perception of threat.[22] It's more surprising to discover the range of physical illnesses that they can cause or exacerbate. Dementia,[23] altered brain function,[24] high blood pressure, heart disease and strokes,[25] lowered resistance to viruses,[26] and even accidents[27] are all more common among chronically lonely people. One study suggests that loneliness has a comparable impact on physical health to smoking fifteen cigarettes a day.[28]

The doctrine has also helped to create what some people describe as a spiritual void: when human life is conceived as a series of transactions, when relationships are recast in purely functional terms, when personal gain counts for everything and pro-social values for nothing, the sense of meaning and purpose is sucked from our lives. We find ourselves in a state of alienation, of anomie, an experience of dislocation that extends beyond the more immediate determinants of mental health.

Our psychological and economic welfare depends on our connection with others. Of all the fantasies human beings entertain, the idea that we can go it alone is the most absurd, and perhaps the most dangerous. We stand together or we fall apart.

11.

INVISIBLE DOCTRINE— INVISIBLE BACKERS

Like Communism, neoliberalism has failed. Yet this zombie doctrine staggers on, protected by a cluster of anonymities. The invisible doctrine of the invisible hand of private interest is sustained by invisible backers.

Over the years, we've begun to discover the identity of some of these patrons. For example, the Institute of Economic Affairs (IEA) in the United Kingdom has, for decades, argued forcibly and publicly against further regulation of tobacco.[1] Since its inception, the IEA insisted it was an independent think tank and reached its conclusions through an objective assessment of the evidence. But in 2013, when tobacco company archives were made public as the result of a legal settlement, some inconvenient information came to light: since 1963 the IEA had been funded by British American Tobacco.[2] It was also being paid by the American multinational tobacco company Philip Morris and Japan Tobacco International.[3]

We've discovered that the Koch brothers—two of the richest people in human history—developed an entire network of "think tanks" to lobby for extreme neoliberalism.[4] Why would they spend so much of their money this way?

There are two likely reasons. The first is immediate self-interest. When David Koch was still alive (he died in 2019), he and his brother Charles owned 84 percent of Koch Industries.[5] This was, at the time of his death, the second-largest private company in the United States. It ran oil refineries, coal suppliers, chemical plants, and logging firms, and turned over roughly $100 billion a year. The brothers each owned assets worth at least $25 billion (in some estimates, considerably more).[6, 7]

Koch Industries has a shocking record of corporate malfeasance and has had to pay tens of millions of dollars in fines and settlements for oil and chemical spills and industrial accidents.[8] Founding and funding lobby groups, which argue that people like them should pay less tax and face fewer rules protecting workers, citizens, and the living world, aligns snugly with their corporate agenda.

But there's more to this than simply smoothing the regulatory pathway for companies such as theirs. People like the Koch brothers buy politics in the way that other oligarchs might buy an island or a yacht—it's an expression of power. This power, however, is closely guarded—and not meant for public display, unlike a luxury yacht, Bugatti sports car, or château on the French Riviera. In setting up one of his lobby groups, Charles Koch, now the surviving brother, noted that "in order to avoid undesirable criticism, the way this organization is controlled and directed should not be widely advertised."[9]

Their spending is an example of what is now commonly referred to as "dark money"[10]: cash whose purpose is to influence political outcomes, but whose sources are not fully disclosed (if at all). This dark money is neoliberalism's fuel. It has propelled its policies into politics, the media, academia, and wider public life.

The Koch brothers have founded or significantly funded more than thirty lobbying groups. They include Americans for Prosperity, the Manhattan Institute, the Cato Institute, the George C. Marshall Institute, the Reason Foundation, and the American Enterprise Institute, to name just a few. These bodies have been instrumental in turning politicians away from environmental laws, social spending, taxes on the rich, and the distribution of wealth. The Kochs have been careful to ensure that their money works for them. "If we're going to give a lot of money," David Koch explained to a sympathetic journalist, "we'll make darn sure they spend it in a way that goes along with our intent. And if they make a wrong turn and start doing things we don't agree with, we withdraw funding."[11]

Through these groups, the two brothers have, arguably, exercised more power than any elected politician in modern history. Take the Heritage Foundation, into which they have poured more than $6 million.[12]

In January 1981, conveniently timed for Ronald Reagan's inauguration, the Heritage Foundation published a work called *Mandate for Leadership*.[13] The document extended to 3,000 pages, across twenty volumes. It contained 2,000 policy proposals, including specific recommendations for reducing the size and scope of some parts of the federal government: those parts that sought to redistribute wealth, defend the poor, and support effective public services. Alongside drastic cuts in tax rates and a scaled-back welfare state, the document proposed greatly enhanced presidential powers and massive increases in military spending. In other words, its avowed mission to "shrink the state" was highly selective—it sought to shrink efforts to improve public welfare, while expanding the government's power over the lives of ordinary citizens. At a cabinet meeting soon after being sworn in, Ronald Reagan handed out copies of *Mandate for Leadership* to everyone in attendance. According to the Heritage Foundation, by the end of the president's first year in office, an astonishing 60 percent of those 2,000 proposals had been implemented.[14]

Around that time, the Koch brothers set up the Mercatus Center at George Mason University in Virginia[15]—yet another think tank that generates and promotes neoliberal ideas. It, too, has exercised astonishing influence over government. For example, fourteen of the twenty-three regulations that President George W. Bush put on the "hit list" of public protections he wanted to revoke were suggested by academics at the Mercatus Center.[16] Bush's concept of the "ownership society"[17, 18]—a neoliberal manifesto transferring responsibility for solving the massive dysfunctions caused by corporate power and state failure to individuals, promoting an extreme conception of property ownership, and cutting tax, regulation, and entitlement programs— like so many of the policies implemented by neoliberal leaders, was devised by another Koch-funded think tank, the Cato Institute.[19, 20]

But the Koch brothers, and oligarchs like them, have not restricted themselves to influencing Republican politicians. Bill Clinton's "Third Way" policies were to a large extent formulated by a lobby group called the Democratic Leadership Council (DLC).[21, 22] Sitting on its executive council were past, present, or future representatives of some of the biggest and most ruthless corporations in the United States, including Enron, Chevron, Texaco, DuPont, Microsoft, IBM, Philip Morris, Verizon Communications, Merck, American Airlines, and, of course, Koch Industries.[23] Two senior Koch executives were members of its board of trustees.[24]

The committee shaped what Clinton and Al Gore called "a new approach to government" that "offers more empowerment and less entitlement . . . that expands opportunity, not bureaucracy."[25] As the language suggests, their "new approach" bore strong similarities to the old approach implemented by Ronald Reagan and George H. W. Bush. The committee's chief executive and "austerity advocate," Bruce Reed, would later become executive director of President Barack Obama's debt commission.[26, 27]

Under such influences, Clinton and Gore continued the neoliberal program by replacing government regulation with "self-regulation." They also introduced sweeping international trade agreements (most notably, and infamously, NAFTA and the World Trade Organization) that accelerated the offshoring of industry and the hollowing-out of American manufacturing industry and the middle class.[28]

But perhaps the most disastrous legacy was Clinton's repeal in 1999, at the urging of neoliberal lobbyists, of the Glass-Steagall Act—legislation introduced in the New Deal era under Franklin Roosevelt in response to the 1929 stock market crash and the Great Depression. The act had separated commercial and financial banks. This was both a vital safeguard against the overwhelming power of the financial sector as well as a firewall impeding the possibility of contagious collapse. Clinton's repeal of the act tore down this firewall, permitting a massive expansion of the financial frontier, which soon followed the classic capitalist pattern of Boom, Bust, Quit. The repeal of Glass-Steagall led directly to the catastrophic bank failures of 2008, and the chaos and financial crises that continue to this day.

It took corporate America a while to warm to Donald Trump. Some of his positions horrified business leaders, especially his hostility toward international trade agreements (the Trans-Pacific Partnership and North American Free Trade Agreement, in particular),[29] the European Union, and NATO. But once he had secured the Republican nomination, the big money began to recognize, in his directionless posturing, an unprecedented opportunity. They came to see his incoherence not as a liability but as an opening—his agenda could easily be shaped. And the dark money network that many American corporations had already developed was perfectly positioned to exploit it.

Trump's team was largely composed of personnel from think tanks funded by the Koch brothers, Exxon, the DonorsTrust (widely seen as the "dark money ATM" of the political right), and other powerful economic interests.[30] In other words, the lobby groups funded by oligarchs and corporations were no longer influencing the government. They *were* the government. Trump's extraordinary plan to cut federal spending by $10.5 trillion was drafted by the Heritage Foundation.[31] They called it, with characteristic audacity, "Blueprint for a New Administration."[32]

Far from keeping his promise to "drain the swamp" of the "lobbyists and corporate stooges working in Washington,"Trump brazenly rescinded Executive Order 13770 on his way out of office[33]—an order that had banned appointees of the administration from lobbying the government for five years or ever working for foreign governments after they had left their posts. Lobbyists and think-tank staff can now cycle freely through government positions, then back to the "private" sphere. This creates a powerful incentive, while they are in office, to give billionaires and private corporations what they want: via this quid pro quo, they're positioning themselves for future employment. In some cases, it's likely to be even more direct: "You cut this regulation and there'll be a lucrative directorship waiting for you when you're out of government." It's an open invitation to corruption. A popular myth holds that Washington, DC, was built on an actual swamp—today, with Trump's help, it has become a political one.

Although Joe Biden sought to position himself as a "transformative president" and champion of the working class and organized labor, he was the favored candidate of big business in the 2020 election. His $1.9 trillion "Build Back Better" program—an economic stimulus package designed to resuscitate a flagging post-pandemic economy—was, in part, a collaborative effort with corporate power. The Business Roundtable association—which consists of more than one hundred CEOs from the likes of Walmart, JPMorgan Chase, and Apple—not only helped to shape the initiative, but also ensured that it was passed. In the words of Michelle Gass, at the time CEO of Kohl's Corporation, "I'm just a big fan of whatever we need to do to help the economy . . . Anything that puts money into the pockets of our consumers is a good thing."

You could see politics as public relations for particular interests. The interests come first—politics is but the means by which they are justified and promoted. The faces may change, but not the influences that shape policy.

12.

ANOMIE IN THE UK

As oligarchs built an infrastructure of persuasion in the United States—from the think tanks, lobby groups, academic institutes, and journalists they had cultivated—on the other side of the Atlantic a corresponding network developed, in some cases funded by the same donors. It began in London in the 1950s, with two fanatical disciples of Friedrich Hayek: Antony Fisher and Oliver Smedley. In 1955 they founded the first of Europe's neoliberal think tanks, the Institute of Economic Affairs. One of the IEA's two founding copresidents, Arthur Seldon, was vice president of Friedrich Hayek's Mont Pelerin Society.[1] The IEA was also one of the publishers of Hayek's *The Road to Serfdom*.

The institute has always insisted that it's an independent, objective body of original thinkers, free from commercial influence. But a note sent from Smedley to Fisher shows how, from the outset, its true purpose was to remain veiled.[2] It was, as Smedley urged, "imperative that we should give no indication in our literature that we are working to educate the Public along certain lines as having a political bias. That is why the first draft [of our aims] is written in rather cagey terms."

The IEA's foundation was "cagey" in more than one sense. Its initial funding came from the fortune that Anthony Fisher had made by importing "broiler chicken farming" (a cruel and abusive farming method that drastically increases productivity) from the United States. Fisher and Smedley collaborated closely with Hayek in establishing the IEA. He advised them not to do any original thinking, but to ensure the institute became a "second-hand dealer in ideas,"[3] promoting the doctrines of the Neoliberal International. It has faithfully followed his script ever since.

Hayek's ideas were at first broadly seen as morally reprehensible. As political scientist Susan George noted,[4] "In 1945 or 1950, if you had seriously proposed any of the ideas and policies in today's standard neoliberal toolkit, you would have been laughed off the stage or sent off to the insane asylum." But Fisher was undeterred and would go on to help found institutes similar to the IEA in other countries,[5] all with the aim of translating Hayek's ideas into a new political common sense. In the process, he helped develop the intellectual framework and justifications upon which the Thatcher and Reagan revolutions were built, honing the arguments that would release the ultra-rich from the democratic constraints—tax, regulations, public opinion—on their freedom to operate. By 2017, the Atlas Network, which Fisher had founded in 1981, was supporting nearly 500 neoliberal think tanks in more than ninety countries.[6] Unsurprisingly, some of the richest people on Earth poured cash into his projects. Notable members of the network include think tanks such as the Institute of Economic Affairs in the United Kingdom; the Cato Institute, Heartland Institute, Heritage Foundation, American Legislative Exchange Council, Manhattan Institute, and Pacific Research Institute in the United States.

Astonishingly, the IEA is still registered as an "educational charity" and lists its official purpose as helping "the general public/mankind."[7] As a result, it is tax exempt. The institute is treated by the BBC and other mainstream media as an independent source of opinion, and its staff—ever-faithful to the neoliberal script—regularly appear on current-affairs programs. Its funding, and on whose behalf it operates, is rarely questioned. It's as if an obscure religious cult had been invited to occupy the nation's most influential platforms to recruit and indoctrinate new followers.

Once Fisher and Smedley had proven the model, other political entrepreneurs began to follow suit. Their work was, and remains, largely shrouded in secrecy. But the autobiography of Madsen Pirie, who cofounded the Adam Smith Institute in 1977, offers a rare glimpse of how they operate.[8] He explains that he built the institute by approaching "all the top companies." About twenty of them responded by reaching for their checkbooks. One enthusiastic supporter was Sir James Goldsmith, an unscrupulous asset stripper (someone who buys companies, sells off their valuable assets, and dissolves what remains). Before making one of his donations, Pirie writes, "he listened carefully as we outlined the project, his eyes twinkling at the audacity and scale of it. Then he had his secretary hand us a check for £12,000 as we left."

Thereafter, Pirie says nothing about the institute's sponsors: like the Institute of Economic Affairs, the Adam Smith Institute refuses to disclose its funding sources.[9] But Pirie's boasts about its achievements are revealing. Every Saturday in the late 1970s, in a London wine bar called the Cork and Bottle, researchers working for Margaret Thatcher—then Leader of the Opposition—convened with leader writers from *The Times* and the *Daily Telegraph*, and staff from the Adam Smith Institute and the Institute of Economic Affairs. Over lunch, they "planned strategy for the week ahead." These meetings, he said, served to "coordinate our activities to make us more effective collectively." The journalists would then turn the institute's proposals into leader columns, while the researchers buttonholed Thatcher's shadow ministers.

As a result, Pirie says, the *Daily Mail* began running a supportive article every time the Adam Smith Institute published something. The paper's editor, David English, oversaw these articles himself and helped the institute to refine its arguments.

Pirie describes how his group devised and polished many of the most important policies implemented by Margaret Thatcher and her successor, John Major. He has claimed (with plenty of supporting evidence) credit for the privatization of the railways and several other public services; for the poll tax (a classic neoliberal flat tax, under which everyone, rich or poor, pays the same amount—its unpopularity forced Thatcher's resignation); for the sale of public housing to private buyers; for the creation of internal markets in education and health; for the establishment of private prisons; and, years later, under the Conservative Chancellor of the Exchequer, George Osborne, for the slashing of taxes paid by the rich.

Pirie also asserts that he wrote the manifesto for the ultra-neoliberal wing of Mrs. Thatcher's government, called *No Turning Back*. Officially, the authors of the document—which was published by the party—were Conservative Members of Parliament such as Michael Forsyth, Peter Lilley, and Michael Portillo.[10] "Nowhere was there any mention of, or connection to, myself or the Adam Smith Institute. They paid me my £1,000 and we were all happy." Pirie's report became the central charter of what we now call Thatcherism, whose Praetorian Guard would brand themselves the "No Turning Back" group.

As successive governments quietly delegate policymaking to opaque, corporate-funded lobby groups, democracy is reduced to a sideshow. The Adam Smith Institute and the IEA are both rated by the accountability group Who Funds You? as "highly opaque"[11]—in other words, they refuse to disclose where their money comes from. But, over the years, investigators have been able to assemble parts of the picture. These think tanks, and others like them, turn out to have been funded by a grim assemblage of billionaires and by oil, coal, chemical, finance, and tobacco companies.

When you ask executives from these think tanks "Who funds you?," they tend to reject the question out of hand, accusing you of "playing the man, not the ball." They also deny that the money they receive has an influence on the positions they take. Given that one of the central tenets of neoliberalism is that human relationships are entirely transactional—motivated above all by the pursuit of money, which shapes our behavior—this claim is, to put it gently, ironic.

Why would corporations and oligarchs wish to spend their money this way? Well, few people would view a tobacco company as a credible source of opinion on public health or a coal company as a neutral commentator on global heating and climate breakdown. So they pay others to pose as neutral commentators and speak on their behalf—this secrecy is essential to the success of the model.

The veteran corporate lobbyist Jeff Judson wrote an essay titled "21 Reasons Why Free-Market Think Tanks Are More Effective than Anyone Else in Changing Public Policy (and One Reason Why They Are Not),"[12] explaining the dark arts he had helped to perfect. Neoliberal think tanks, he remarked, are "the source of many of the ideas and facts that appear in countless editorials, news articles, and syndicated columns." They have "considerable influence and close personal relationships with elected officials." They "support and encourage one another, echo and amplify their messages, and can pull together . . . coalitions on the most important public policy issues."

But their most important advantage, Judson noted, is as follows. Companies that admit to being lobbyists—in other words, those that are listed as public relations agencies or reputation launderers—"work for specific clients who operate at the mercy of a regulator or lawmaker." This makes them "vulnerable to retribution for daring to criticize or speak out." Think tanks, on the other hand, "are virtually immune to retribution . . . Donors are confidential. The identity of donors to think tanks is protected from involuntary disclosure." His essay, published online, has since been deleted.

In this way, those who fund think tanks are shielded from democratic scrutiny. Companies and oligarchs whose lobbying activities might otherwise be a cause for public uproar quietly insert their demands into the political conversation through their well-funded proxies. As a consultant who worked for the Koch brothers expressed it, they see the funding of think tanks "as a way to get things done without getting dirty themselves."[13]

This leads us to a crucial concept, without which it is impossible to understand modern politics. We call it the "Pollution Paradox." It goes as follows:

> The dirtiest, most antisocial and damaging companies have the greatest incentive to invest in politics, as they are the ones most likely to face the heaviest regulation, if exposed to full democratic scrutiny. For this reason, they spend more money on changing political outcomes than any other commercial interests. The result is that politics comes to be dominated by the dirtiest, most antisocial and damaging industries.

The Pollution Paradox helps to explain a wide range of otherwise inexplicable phenomena, including the sustained failure by wealthy and technologically advanced governments to prevent our rush toward disaster: to arrest climate and ecological breakdown; to protect public health; to tackle the crisis of obesity (whose incidence has tripled worldwide since the mid-1970s[14] and is driven, above all, by the sale and marketing of junk food); to curtail the financial sector's predatory and destabilizing strategies; to avert such avoidable catastrophes as London's Grenfell Tower disaster and freight-train wrecks in the American Midwest; to regulate waste disposal and reduce organized crime's influence and control over the sector; to stop the pollution of our rivers and our drinking water; to curtail the ransacking of our seas by the fishing industry; or to resist the highly exploitative labor relations that have returned to dominate many service and manufacturing sectors.

Scarcely anyone in our societies welcomes these shifts. If the policies enabling them were put to the vote, they would be soundly rejected. Why, then, do so many of the world's governments remain committed to them? Because anti-social industries—those with the most to lose—invest the most in politics.

The most effective tool for promoting the interests of dirty and damaging industries is the Neoliberal International—its network of think tanks, academic departments, journalists, and government advisers. As we've seen, it has the capacity to formulate government policy, find the words to make the outrageous sound like common sense ("Unless the right to strike is rescinded, we'll never compete with China," "The wealthier those at the top become, the more the rising tide will lift all boats"), and create the impression in the media that there are two sides to even the starkest forms of exploitation ("The minimum wage inhibits job creation," "The rules preventing river pollution will stop the homes we need from being built"). It helps ensure that the Pollution Paradox continues to dominate our politics.

The confusions of neoliberalism mesh with the namelessness and placelessness of modern capitalism. Consider the franchise model, which ensures that many workers have no idea whom they are laboring for.[15] Consider the network of offshore tax havens and secrecy regimes, which disguise their beneficiaries so effectively that even the police can't figure out who they are.[16] Consider the tax arrangements designed by lawyers working for oligarchs and corporations, which bamboozle even governments. Consider the complex financial products that nobody understands, like those that helped create the financial meltdown of 2008.

The anonymities of neoliberalism are fiercely guarded. Those who follow the doctrines of Hayek, von Mises, and Friedman now reject the term "neoliberalism"—arguing that it is used only pejoratively. Philip Magness, writing for the American Institute of Economic Research, for example, says: "The term neoliberalism is probably the trendiest scapegoat in intellectual circles . . . For a movement with next to zero actual claimants, neoliberalism attracts an inordinate amount of scorn, much of it viciously profane and spiteful."[17]

The former chief editor of the *New Republic*, Jonathan Chait, has argued the term has become an all-purpose insult, "an attempt to win an argument with an epithet."[18]

They have a point—today, for the most part, "neoliberalism" is used derisively. But it was the term neoliberals coined to describe their own doctrine, and they've offered us no alternative with which to replace it. In fact, they tend to reject the notion that neoliberalism is a distinct ideology that needs a name at all. This is part of the effort to normalize and naturalize it, to persuade us that it is just the way things are, and the only way they can be.

To recap, neoliberalism's network of influence operates as follows:

- Oligarchs and corporations often covertly (i.e., using "dark money") fund think tanks and academic departments.

- These institutions, in turn, make the unreasonable demands of the oligarchs and corporations sound reasonable and normal.

- The press—also largely controlled by oligarchs—presents these policy proposals as critical and important insights by independent organizations, creating the impression that people in different places are spontaneously coming to the same conclusions on the basis of sound, disinterested research.

- Politicians who are paid by, or sympathetic to, the oligarchs and corporations cite the press coverage as evidence of public demand.

- The voice of the oligarchs is interpreted as the voice of the people.

In April 1938, President Franklin Roosevelt sent Congress this warning: "The liberty of a democracy is not safe if the people tolerate the growth of private power to a point where it becomes stronger than their democratic state itself. That, in its essence, is fascism."[19] It is a warning we would do well to remember.

13.

LYING THROUGH THEIR TEETH

Given the broad unpopularity of their proposals, neoliberals need to choose their targets carefully. Some public services, which are obscure or poorly understood by the voters, can be privatized easily and with little controversy. Others, those more valued and understood, must be privatized more stealthily. Certain moves must remain hidden or imposed at a moment of crisis when we are least able to respond.

Among the most treasured of public services in the United Kingdom is the National Health Service (NHS). It is seen as one of the country's proudest achievements—a service free at the point of use, which, at its peak, ensured that the care the poor received was as good as the care the rich received. When the NHS was established in 1948, for the first time in our history people were assured they wouldn't have to die needlessly of treatable diseases or bankrupt themselves in paying for medicines or surgery. The NHS took pride of place in the opening ceremony of the 2012 London Olympics—the one thing, in this divided nation, on which everyone could agree.

Well, perhaps not *everyone*. For years, the neoliberal think tanks—while refusing to say whether they were, as many suspect, being funded by private health and insurance companies—have argued for the privatization of the NHS.[1] But even they have been unable to persuade us that this policy would improve our lives. No government has dared implement it, overtly at least. Instead, governments have pursued another means to achieve the same ends—death by a thousand cuts.

It is generally recognized by health professionals around the world that to keep pace with an aging population and technological change, a modern healthcare system requires an annual 4 percent real terms increase in funding.[2] Anything less results in a steady erosion of the service. Neoliberal governments have systematically underfunded the NHS, providing an average annual 1.2 percent instead.[3] The cumulative NHS funding gap—the difference between the 4 percent it needs and the money it receives—has risen to more than £200 billion since the Conservatives came to power in 2010. As a result, almost 9,000 general and acute beds have been lost in England in the past decade.[4] Whereas the Organisation for Economic Co-operation and Development (OECD) average is five beds per 1,000 people, the UK capacity is less than half, at 2.4.[5]

But funding cuts alone are a slow way to kill a service. You need accelerants, and the most effective of them is the disempowerment, frustration, and elimination of the staff providing the service. Across the NHS, doctors and nurses are leaving in droves, as the pay is so poor, conditions so dangerous, and the stress intolerable. But in some sectors, governments have found even quicker ways to evict them. NHS dentistry has become the template for the destruction of the rest of the service.

In principle, every child in the UK is entitled to free treatment by an NHS dentist, as are people on benefits, pregnant women, and those who have recently given birth. In theory, they all have free and full access to the service. But that service no longer exists: 80 percent of dental practices in the UK are no longer taking on new child NHS patients and about 90 percent are refusing new adult patients.[6]

There's no mystery about why the service is vanishing— successive governments have ensured that if dentists treat patients on the NHS, they *lose money*. Since 2006, dentists have worked for the NHS under a contract so ridiculous that it seems designed to fail. They are paid according to "units of dental activity" (UDA), which bear no relation to the costs of treatment.[7] Every practice has to meet an annual UDA target. There is no incentive to practice preventive dentistry and every incentive to exclude the patients with the greatest needs. Nor is there any encouragement for dentists to seek further training and qualifications: they are paid at the UDA rate, regardless of skills and experience.[8] So, if you work for the NHS, you can kiss career progression goodbye.

To make matters worse, while dental inflation—driven by the rising costs of lab bills, energy, wages, and materials— is about 11 percent a year,[9] the funding for NHS dental services has been cut in real terms by 4 percent a year.[10]

Broadly speaking, the only dentists still working in the NHS are those who feel a moral obligation to do so, despite losing money and working longer hours. They end up subsidizing their NHS treatments through their private work.

The destruction of NHS dentistry can be seen as an experiment—a successful experiment whose results can now be applied to other services. It works like this: rather than inciting public fury by announcing a change of policy, you proclaim your undying commitment to the service while starving it of funds until it collapses. People may grumble and (unwisely) gnash their teeth, but they don't rise up. Already struggling with the deficiencies of public services that have been stripped of funds, most of us find even the thought of joining yet another advocacy campaign to be exhausting.

The result, in one of the richest nations on Earth, is that people are extracting their own teeth,[11] making their own fillings, improvising dentures and sticking them to their gums with superglue, and overdosing on painkillers.[12] Those who can afford to pay for private treatment will do so; those who cannot will face pain and misery. These appalling outcomes may appear to be accidents of policy, but the policy is deliberate. What the UK's ultra-neoliberal government has done to dentistry is what it wishes on the rest of the NHS. But the components of the service must be extracted tooth by tooth.

Across neoliberal states, valued services are destroyed by similar means. In the United States, Republican governments have waged war on a wide range of entitlement programs: Medicaid, the Social Services Block Grant Program, the Supplemental Nutrition Assistance Program (SNAP), the Temporary Assistance for Needy Families, support for after-school programs and improvements in school instruction, the Community Services Block Grant, the Community Development Block Grant Programs, home heating assistance for low-income households, housing programs including HOME and Choice Neighborhoods. It's no accident that the US is currently facing a crisis in homelessness. Rather than providing low-income people with support of the kind that could help them to escape from poverty—job training, childcare, adequate nutrition, and health care—Donald Trump and his administration pulled the rug out from under them, with the inevitable result that many have been driven toward destitution.[13]

The Trump administration also set out to ensure that government institutions failed. Alongside massive tax cuts, which included a plunge in the corporate tax rate from 35 percent to 21 percent,[14] he proposed deep cuts to the Departments of Labor, State, Justice, Housing and Urban Development, Education, and Transportation, as well as the Office of Foreign Assistance and the US Army Corps of Engineers. He slashed the Internal Revenue Service, limiting its ability to collect the taxes that were still owed. He also sought to gut federal science agencies, including the Environmental Protection Agency and the Department of the Interior, and to interfere with their scientific advisory panels. All in all, nearly 100 environmental rules were officially reversed, revoked, or rolled back under

Trump[15]—including the Clean Power Plan, Endangered Species Act, Coal Ash Rule, and Mercury and Air Toxic Standards.

Trump boasted about liberating the United States from the 2016 Paris Agreement on Climate Change and opened a record amount of public land to drilling and mining. But, like Ronald Reagan and the Heritage Foundation, his mission to "shrink the state" was highly selective: he added $133 billion to the 2017–19 defense budgets—a staggering 23 percent increase.[16] Even military commanders and experts questioned the logic of this expenditure, in a nation that already spends more than the next eight countries combined, three times more than China, and ten times more than Russia.[17]

Trump came to power through a popular backlash against neoliberalism's crushing of political choice and its devastating impacts on public well-being. But the paradoxical result was to elevate just the kind of man that Hayek worshipped. Trump, who has no coherent politics, is the perfect representation of Hayek's "independent"; the beneficiary of inherited wealth, unconstrained by common morality, whose gross predilections strike a new path that others may follow. Vain and easily influenced, he quickly became the neoliberals' most valuable and malleable asset. Even so, the Neoliberal International would not have to wait long before finding an even more effective vehicle for its ambitions.

14.

WHEN NEOLIBERALS GET EVERYTHING THEY WANT: A CASE STUDY

Let's take a look at what happens when neoliberals are able to do everything they've dreamed of. In September 2022, Liz Truss became prime minister of the United Kingdom. She was the most unrestrained neoliberal ever to have assumed high office in the UK. Her views made even her hero Margaret Thatcher look moderate.

Liz Truss was the co-author of a book called *Britannia Unchained*,[1] a semi-literate polemic that transferred the blame for everything that had gone wrong in the UK to "a diminished work ethic and a culture of excuses." It blamed inequality and the lack of social mobility in the country not on the neoliberalism that had delivered them, but on "laziness." Citing no meaningful evidence, it maintained that "once they enter the workplace, the British are among the worst idlers in the world." It celebrated the "black-market buccaneers" who in other countries have created "a lawless place" where demand can be instantly met by supply. This, Truss and her coauthors insisted, is "the purest level of entrepreneurialism, untouched by law, regulation or tax." The book provided a terrifying, dystopian vision of a nation governed by raw economic power, without effective social or environmental protection.

To a greater extent than those of any previous leader, Truss's politics were shaped by dark money neoliberal think tanks. According to the head of the Institute of Economic Affairs, before she became prime minister, she had spoken at more of its events than "any other politician over the past twelve years."[2] In 2011, Truss founded the Free Enterprise Group (FEG) of Conservative MPs, which appeared to be a kind of subsidiary of the IEA. The FEG webpage was registered by the IEA's director Ruth Porter.[3] The IEA organized events for the group and supplied it with media briefings.[4] If you tried to open its webpage, you were redirected to the Free Market Forum, which calls itself "a project of the Institute of Economic Affairs."[5]

In 2022, Truss had the opportunity to put her beliefs into practice. In campaigning to become the leader of the Conservative Party, she published what she called her "Plan for Growth."[6] It was pure neoliberal gospel: "cut taxes now, unshackle business from burdensome regulation, implement supply side reform . . . create new, low-tax, low-regulation investment zones."

Conservative Party leaders—who, if the Conservatives are in power, automatically become prime minister—are chosen solely by the party's MPs and members. At the time, there were roughly 200,000 members, disproportionately rich, white, old, male, and living in the south of England. As soon as Truss won this less-than-democratic "election" for PM, she began unleashing her agenda. She announced proposals to cut taxes for the rich, scrap England's anti-obesity measures,[7] remove the cap on bankers' bonuses, rip down the planning controls that prevent urban sprawl, expunge 570 environmental laws,[8] and create "investment zones"—otherwise known as free ports.[9]

These free ports are places in which the usual rules don't apply, and citizens have less decision-making power. They're the equivalent of the royal forests of medieval England. "Forest," in fact, derives from the Latin *foris*, which means "outside": outside the usual laws of the land. The forests were hunting estates where the king's private interests overrode the rights of the common people. In crucial respects, these "special economic zones" operate as if they were outside a nation's borders.

To ensure that any inconvenient public opposition would be minimized, Truss then pushed the Public Order Bill through Parliament, whose purpose was to crush protest. It is the most repressive legislation introduced to the UK in the modern era,[10] lending credence to the long-held observation that the more unequal a society becomes, the more oppressive its laws must be. To implement her program, she filled key government posts with staff from neoliberal think tanks (much as Trump had done). Ruth Porter from the IEA, who had set up Truss's Free Enterprise Group, became her senior special adviser. At the IEA, Porter had called for a long list of neoliberal policies, including reducing housing and child benefits, charging patients to use the NHS, cutting overseas aid, and scrapping green funds.[11]

Truss's chief economic adviser was Matthew Sinclair,

formerly chief executive of the Taxpayers' Alliance, another neoliberal think tank funded obscurely by foreign donors.[12] He was the author of a book called *Let Them Eat Carbon*, which argued against taking action to prevent climate breakdown. Among other astonishing claims, it maintained that "equatorial regions might suffer, but it is entirely possible that this will be balanced out by areas like Greenland."[13] In other words, let's trade the lives of billions of people in the tropics against the prospects of some of the least inhabited places on Earth.

Truss's political secretary, Sophie Jarvis, was head of government affairs at the Adam Smith Institute. Two weeks after Truss became prime minister, she and the chancellor of the exchequer, Kwasi Kwarteng, devised what was deceptively billed as a "mini-budget." In reality—though short on detail, short on funding, and even shorter on thinking—it would have a mega-impact. It sought definitively to reset the relationship between the rich and the rest. With one fell swoop, it abolished the top rate of income tax, cut the basic rate, and canceled or abandoned a long list of other progressive taxes.

On the day of the budget, the think tanks crowed about their takeover of the government. The founder of the Conservative Home website, Tim Montgomerie, remarked that this was "a massive moment" for the Institute of Economic Affairs, which had "incubated Truss and Kwarteng during their early years as MPs. Britain is now their laboratory." The head of the institute, Mark Littlewood, retweeted his comment with a sunglasses emoji.[14]

Above a screenshot of a *Guardian* headline asking, "Has

Liz Truss Handed Power Over to the Extreme Neoliberal Thinktanks?," the IEA's head of public policy, Matthew Lesh, wrote: "Yes."[15] He published a list of the many IEA demands that found their way into her budget.[16]

But it took less than a day for the edifice to collapse in a heap of dust. The financial sector recoiled in fear. The pound tanked, forcing the Bank of England to intervene. Truss's tax cuts, combined with the higher interest rates and borrowing costs resulting from her kamikaze budget, cost the country around £30 billion.[17] A month after the budget was announced, and a mere forty-nine days after having taken office, Liz Truss found herself with no choice but to resign—with poetic justice, brought down by the very "markets" she had claimed to serve. Hers was the shortest premiership in British history.

The public response? Truss began and ended her term with the lowest approval rating on record[18]—driving some of the worst polling results the Conservative Party had ever seen.[19] The think tanks that had designed and propagated her policies frantically sought to distance themselves, blaming the disaster on "poor implementation" or "incompleteness." But we should see Truss's government as an experiment: What happens when neoliberal ultras, backed and advised by dark money think tanks, get everything they want?

Answer: Economic life falls off a cliff.

15.

ATTACK OF THE KILLER CLOWNS

Not many years ago, comedians complained that politicians had become so boring that they were no longer worth satirizing. Today, they have the opposite problem: the satirists can't keep up. The dull, gray political leaders of the 1990s and early twenty-first century have been replaced in many nations by outrageous and absurd exhibitionists.

Italy's Silvio Berlusconi—charismatic, provocative, and populist—was the pioneer and archetype of the new political model. But similar characters soon came to the fore: Donald Trump (US), Boris Johnson (UK), Jair Bolsonaro (Brazil), Scott Morrison (Australia), Narendra Modi (India), Benjamin Netanyahu (Israel), Rodrigo Duterte (Philippines), Recep Erdogan (Turkey), Viktor Orbán (Hungary), Javier Milei (Argentina), Geert Wilders (the Netherlands). Deeply flawed human beings with oversized egos and pathological insecurities have risen to dominate politics in many of the world's democracies. This is the age of the killer clowns.

These "mavericks" are distinguished by buffoonery, shamelessness, and a flaunting disregard for justice, due process, and political standards. They come to power by stoking outrage. They loudly pledge, on behalf of "the people," to disrupt the old, corrupt political order. Invariably, however, once they take power, corruption and nepotism prosper as never before.

No such person comes to power without the consent of capital. So the obvious question is "Why?" Why are the ultra-rich—who previously used their money and media to promote reliable, charisma-free politicians—now funding this three-ring circus? Why did they want to support middle managers one moment and jesters the next? The reason is that the nature of capitalism has changed.

During the 1990s and early 2000s, the dominant political force in neoliberal nations was corporate power. What corporate power wanted was technocratic government. It wanted competent managers who could deliver a stable state platform for business and secure their profits against democratic change. This force still exists, of course. Corporate power remains a great influence on government and a constraint upon democracy. But it has been mutating into, and become overlain by, another force: oligarchic power.

This mutation results from one of the paradoxes of neoliberalism mentioned in chapter 7: while it fetishizes competitive enterprise, in reality it empowers rentiers and asset strippers—the opposite of the creative entrepreneurs it celebrates. It has enabled the spiral of patrimonial wealth accumulation, described by Thomas Piketty in *Capital in the Twenty-First Century*,[1] to turn ever faster: those who are rich today become, through their economic and political power, even richer tomorrow. Those who are poor today, regardless of their hard work or creative talents, are likely to remain poor.

Many of today's oligarchs achieved their position through corporate power. As taxes for the very rich were curtailed, trade unions hobbled, and workers' wage demands suppressed, owners and chief executives were—thanks to soaring "compensation" packages—transformed from very rich to obscenely and unimaginably rich. The gains that had once been more widely distributed within the corporation became increasingly concentrated in their hands. From the pupal stage of the old dominant class, an even more powerful class emerged and took flight.

When we say "oligarch," you doubtless picture a Russian (perhaps lying on the deck of a luxury yacht, eating Beluga caviar, sipping fine vodka, and accompanied by minimally attired "elite companions"). But there are now oligarchs—people whose inordinate economic power translates into inordinate political power—in every society. Rupert Murdoch is an oligarch. So are Charles Koch, and the hedge-fund manager Robert Mercer, and Elon Musk, and Jeff Bezos, and Mark Zuckerberg, and the Indian billionaire Gautam Adani, and so on.

What oligarchs want is not, in the main, what the old corporations wanted. In the words of their favored enforcer Steve Bannon, they seek the "deconstruction of the administrative state."[2] Chaos is the profit multiplier for the disaster capitalism on which the billionaires thrive. Every rupture is used to seize more of the assets on which our lives depend. The pandemonium of Berlusconi's Italy, the repeated meltdowns and shutdowns of government under Trump—these are "deconstructions" of the kind that benefit Friedrich Hayek's "independents."

Broadly speaking, there are now two main forms of capitalist enterprise. The first could be described as "housebroken capitalism." This domesticated version—companies whose investments might not mature for several years, that rely on certainty and continuity—seeks an accommodation with the administrative state, and benefits from stability, predictability, and the regulations that exclude dirtier and rougher competitors. It can coexist with the light intervention that accompanies a weak form of democracy. The manufacturing and agricultural sectors, for instance, rely on a stable regulatory environment, as well as consistent government policies, such as trade agreements, subsidies, and tax incentives.

The second could be described as "warlord capitalism." This sees all restraints on wealth accumulation—including taxes, regulations, and the public ownership of essential services—as illegitimate. Nothing should be allowed to stand in the way of profit-making. Warlord capitalists promote what they call "liberty"—in other words, Hayek's "freedom from coercion": total freedom for themselves at everyone else's expense. Although housebroken capitalism versus warlord capitalism does not map neatly onto corporate versus oligarchic power, there are clear overlaps.

Occasionally, the warlord capitalists and their political backers say the quiet bit out loud. Peter Thiel, the co-founder of PayPal and Palantir, once confessed: "I no longer believe that freedom and democracy are compatible."[3]

Mike Lee, senior Republican senator for Utah, stated that "democracy isn't the objective" of the US political system, "liberty, peace, and prosperity are."[4] Hayek, as we have already seen, expressed a preference for Pinochet's dictatorship over what he called "a democratic government devoid of liberalism." The very rich are singing from his hymn book.

We find ourselves caught in the crossfire of a civil war within capitalism. Among its many outcomes is "Brexit"— the UK's departure from the European Union.

Brexit has provided an astonishing opportunity for warlord capitalism. It is a chance not just to rip up specific, inconvenient rules, but also to tear down the uneasy truce between capitalism and democracy. Peter Hargreaves of the financial-services business Hargreaves Lansdown, a billionaire who donated £3.2 million to the pro-Brexit "Leave.EU" campaign,[5] explained that after the UK had left the European Union, "We will get out there and we will become incredibly successful because we will be insecure again. And insecurity is fantastic."[6] For men like Hargreaves, insecurity is opportunity. He uses the word "we" three times in the first sentence, but it does not mean the same in every instance. "*We* the oligarchs" will become incredibly successful because "*we* who are not oligarchs" will be insecure again.

The chaos caused by Brexit has become its own justification: times are tough, so we must slash regulations and liberate business to make us rich again. This new fire-front has burned through the governments that sought to implement it, but also through many of the restraints on the most brutal forms of capitalism. Brexit's backers have sought to tear down environmental, labor, human rights, and consumer protections.

Housebroken capitalists were justifiably horrified by Brexit. Immediately before the referendum on whether to leave the European Union in June 2016, some 1,280 business leaders, including executives from among the oldest companies listed on the FTSE 100 Index, signed a letter to *The Times* warning that "Britain leaving the EU would mean uncertainty for our firms, less trade with Europe and fewer jobs."[7] Not only has Brexit created turbulence and uncertainty, and dampened economic activity in general, but it has undermined the market advantages for businesses that play by the rules. Without regulatory constraints, the warlords would wipe them out. In response to concerns expressed by the Confederation of British Industry (at the time the most august institution of housebroken capital), Boris Johnson made a remark that might previously have seemed unthinkable, coming from the mouth of a senior Conservative: "Fuck business."[8]

Understood in this light, Brexit was scarcely about the UK at all. Oligarchs who have shown great interest in the subject tend to have weak or partial ties to Britain. According to Andy Wigmore of Leave.EU, the campaign received significant assistance from the US billionaire and *Breitbart News* owner, Robert Mercer.[9] By far the biggest individual donors to the Brexit Party, which pursued the hardest of possible exits, were Christopher Harborne,[10] who is based in Thailand,[11] and Jeremy Hosking,[12] who has businesses listed in Dublin and Delaware. The newspaper owners who went to such lengths to make Brexit happen are domiciled offshore. For people like Rupert Murdoch, the United Kingdom must look like a beachhead among the richest and most powerful of nations. Turning Chile or Indonesia into a giant free port is one thing. The UK is a much bigger prize.

None of this, of course, is what the people of the United Kingdom were told they were voting for. Those who fronted the campaign—people like Boris Johnson and Nigel Farage—were human smoke bombs, generating a camouflaging cloud of xenophobia and culture wars. They pitted "us" against "them." Leavers were "true patriots" who claimed to be "taking back control"—reasserting state sovereignty and limiting immigration—against "elitist" cosmopolitan liberals happy to surrender national autonomy to faceless Eurocrats. In doing so, they provided cover for the economic warfare being waged by disaster capitalists. The persistent trick of modern politics is to disguise economic and political conflicts as cultural conflicts. Throughout this saga, the media reported the diversion, not the maneuvers; the noise, not the signal.

As this example suggests, the killer clowns offer the oligarchs two other powerful tools: distraction and exhaustion. While the very rich fleece us, we are persuaded to look elsewhere. The buffoons first mesmerize us, then channel the anger that should be reserved for plutocrats and political corruption toward immigrants, women, Jews, Muslims, Black and Brown people, and other imaginary enemies. At the same time, their flamboyant lies and deliberate outrages, the twenty-four-hour news-cycle churn of manufactured scandals, exhaust our capacity to respond.

It's all too much. The noise overwhelms the signal, the sensory overload short-circuits our capacity for agency. Weary and depleted, we tune out . . . and withdraw from political action.

16.

CONSPIRACY FICTIONS

"**S**unlight," as US Supreme Court justice Louis Brandeis proclaimed over a century ago, "is the best disinfectant." Transparency and good governance are essential to democracy. If we don't understand who and what we're voting for, we end up—as so many have done across the ages—casting votes against our own interests.

The aims and strategies of neoliberalism are, when seen and understood, immensely unpopular. So how do the self-serving ideologues put the genie of public knowledge back in its bottle? How do they prevent us from understanding what is happening and why? One of their most powerful tools is what is widely known as the "conspiracy theory."

But the term "conspiracy theory" is a misnomer. There are plenty of genuine conspiracies: powerful people coming together, hidden from public view, to advance their own interests. This is how power operates, and always has. This book mentions several of these conspiracies. When those who already possess power and wealth want more of it, they don't advertise their agenda—let alone the means of going about it.

What we tend to call "conspiracy theories" are actually *conspiracy fictions*. Conspiracy fictions are stories about *alleged* conspiracies for which there is no evidence. Often, they're contradicted by abundant evidence. In many cases they have already been debunked. Almost invariably, those who peddle conspiracy fictions have no interest whatever in genuine conspiracies—the true machinations of power—aside from creating cover for them.

Why is there so little overlap between those who promote conspiracy fictions and those who investigate genuine conspiracies? We suspect there might be several reasons. One of them is ownership—to peddle conspiracy fictions and persuade others to believe them is, in itself, an assertion of power.

Another is reassurance. This might sound odd, since these fictions purport to reveal "the terrifying truth!"—but oftentimes their message is not terrifying at all. On the contrary, they can be as reassuring as a lullaby. They tell people that all is basically well: that our fears are unfounded. Climate breakdown? "It's a hoax." Covid? "Nothing to worry about." Power? "It's just a tiny cabal of Jews." Instead of huge, structural forces that present daunting existential threats, the purveyors of conspiracy fictions tell their audience that the "real" villains are people who wield little real power—such as climate scientists, town planners, public-health researchers, teachers, librarians, or even Anthony Fauci (former chief medical adviser to the US president). It's even more reassuring when the scapegoats have no political power at all—ordinary citizens who are asylum seekers, or who are Muslim, or Jewish, or Black, or Brown, or Asian, or queer, or trans, or women.

There's a further reason, which may be the most important of all. Conspiracy fictions tell people, in effect, that they don't have to do anything. They rob us of agency, and that's part of the attraction. If the problem is a remote and highly unlikely "other"—rather than a system in which we are deeply embedded, which cannot be changed without a democratic campaign of resistance and reconstruction—you can wash your hands of it and get on with your life. So, in promoting conspiracy fictions, you get the best of all possible worlds: self-aggrandizement, reassurance, and freedom from civic responsibility. This may explain why those who take an interest in conspiracy fictions are often so uninterested in genuine conspiracies.

But there is a danger in making conspiracy fictions sound like a harmless hobby. While the reasons for their popularity—and the stories themselves—can often be remarkably petty, they can also take us toward a dark place. This is because, regardless of where they originate, successful conspiracy fictions almost always land with the far right. Conspiracy fictions are the fuel of far-right politics: it cannot operate without them.

These fictions are also the portal through which many people—often from surprisingly progressive political backgrounds—migrate into far-right politics. We've witnessed this phenomenon, in particular, among New Age and alternative movements,[1] which are generally associated with left and green politics.

There has long been an overlap between certain New Age and far-right ideas. The Nazis embraced astrology, pagan festivals, organic farming, forest conservation, ecological education, and nature worship. They promoted homeopathy and "natural healing," and tended to resist vaccination.[2] We should be aware of this history, but without indulging in what the historian Simon Schama calls the "obscene syllogism":[3] the idea that because the Nazis promoted New Age beliefs, alternative medicine, and ecological protection, anyone who does so is also a Nazi. But much of what we are seeing at the moment is new. A few years ago, dreadlocked hippies spreading QAnon lies and denying climate science would have seemed unthinkable. Today, the old boundaries have broken down, as a wide range of people grow increasingly susceptible to right-wing narratives.

The anti-vaccine movement has proven to be an effective channel for pumping far-right ideas into left-wing countercultures.[4] For several years, anti-vax has straddled the green left and the far right. Trump flirted with it, at one point inviting the anti-vaxxer Robert F. Kennedy Jr. to chair a "commission on vaccination safety and scientific integrity."[5] (Robert F. Kennedy Jr., at the time of this writing, has recently abandoned the Democratic Party to run as an independent for president of the United States.) Skepticism toward the power and purpose of Big Pharma is entirely reasonable. But in some quarters it has morphed into a suspicion of all preventative medicine, however necessary and effective. Ancient links between "wellness" movements and antisemitic paranoia have, in some cases, been forged anew. The notion of the "sovereign body," untainted by chemical contamination, has begun to fuse with the fear that a shadowy cabal is trying to deprive us of autonomy.[6]

Conspiracy fictions have been used as a political weapon for millennia, diverting popular discontent toward scapegoats: Jews, "witches," "saboteurs," immigrants, ethnic minorities, socialists, communists. Conspiracy fictions have led, throughout the span of human history, to pogroms, massacres, torture, and genocide—as those who are subject to them, inevitably, become targets for violence. Today, micro-targeting on social media, peer-to-peer texting, deepfakes, and other digital tools accelerate the generation and spread of these fictions, sowing confusion and creating alternative realities faster than ever before.

The more we learn, the more we discover how much of the fury and loathing directed toward innocent people has been manufactured and paid for. In the 2016 EU referendum campaign, the 2016 US presidential general election, and the campaign that brought Jair Bolsonaro to power in Brazil in 2019, we saw how effective groundless scare stories can be in generating support for elite political projects. People who peddle conspiracy fictions might imagine they are "sticking it to the Man." In reality, they are lending him a hand.

The Tea Party movement, launched in February 2009, mobilized unwitting participants against what was characterized as an "elite power grab." By this, they were referring to Barack Obama's healthcare reforms, climate policies, and other attempts—feeble and diluted as they were—to roll back the most obscene excesses of neoliberalism.

The official version of events claims that the movement was launched by CNBC reporter Rick Santelli, who called from the floor of the Chicago Mercantile Exchange for traders to hold a "Tea Party" to dump derivative securities (a kind of complex financial instrument) in Lake Michigan, in order to stop Obama's plan to "subsidize the losers."[7] By losers, Santelli meant people struggling to keep their homes in the wake of the subprime mortgage crisis. Even at face value, it was a telling call: a bankers' revolt against the undeserving poor. But the reality was even darker.

The movement looked like, and claimed to be, a spontaneous uprising of concerned citizens. In reality, it was largely engineered by Americans for Prosperity (AFP),[8] yet another organization founded and funded by the Koch brothers. AFP provided the Tea Party movement's key organizing tools. The moment Santelli started speaking on the floor of the Chicago Mercantile Exchange, Americans for Prosperity launched its Tea Party Facebook page and started organizing Tea Party events: none of it was coincidental.

Interviewed by *New York* magazine, David Koch stated, "I've never been to a Tea Party event. No one representing the Tea Party has ever even approached me."[9] Film footage, however, clearly contradicts this claim, showing him at the Americans for Prosperity's 2009 "Defending the Dream" summit.[10] "Five years ago," he told the delegates, "my brother Charles and I provided the funds to start Americans for Prosperity. It's beyond my wildest dreams how AFP has grown into this enormous organization." As a series of AFP organizers stepped up to proclaim how they had set up dozens of Tea Party events in their home states, he nodded and beamed from the podium like a C-suite executive receiving rosy reports from his regional sales directors. Afterward, the delegates dispersed into AFP workshops, where they were trained in how to organize and run further Tea Party events.

The Tea Party, in other words, was classic Astroturf: an operation that purports to be a spontaneously organized grassroots movement, but in reality is founded, funded, and facilitated by elite interests.

The Tea Party movement would become the organizational focus of resistance to the Obama presidency. It generated or spread some of the most potent conspiracy fictions deployed against him, unleashed a new wave of culture wars themes and tactics, mobilized racism and white supremacism, and galvanized the radical right[11]— leading both to Trump and to the irreconcilable differences that now divide America.

As one of the Koch brothers' former consultants explained, "The Koch brothers gave the money that founded [the Tea Party]. It's like they put the seeds in the ground. Then the rainstorm comes, and the frogs come out of the mud—and they're our candidates!"[12] The deployment of conspiracy fictions, such as the "birther" myth alleged against Barack Obama (falsely claiming that he was not a natural-born US citizen), is a classic example of the way this tactic is used to disarm those who oppose—however ineffectually—plutocratic power. The great irony here is that fake stories about shadowy elites are routinely propagated by bona fide shadowy elites, such as the Koch brothers and their Americans for Prosperity network. These fake stories are used to divert attention from genuine conspiracies: a tactic Steve Bannon, always ready to boast about his dark arts, called "flooding the zone with shit."[13] The tactic has been deployed to great effect by supporters of neoliberalism, as well as the demagogues that neoliberalism has spawned.

Dominic Cummings—who performed the same role for Boris Johnson and the oligarchs dominating UK politics as Steve Bannon did for Trump and the oligarchs in the US—spent his time behind the wheel persuading us that we could "take back control" from the "elites." But the "elites" we were being induced to fear were not the rich and powerful. The true enemies of progress in this demonology were teachers, professors, left-wing journalists, trade-union organizers, Black activists, environmental campaigners, public intellectuals, and independent thinkers. After the parties of the left fell into line with corporate power, the right seized the language they had abandoned. Now we see an almost perfect language swap. Parties that once belonged on the left talk about "security" and "stability," whereas those on the right talk of "liberation" and "revolt."

Everything is inverted. We are induced to believe that the real threats to our prosperity and freedom arise not from economic power, but from "woke" academics and campaigners. Refugees, typically the most vulnerable and powerless people in any society, are presented as a mortal threat to our "way of life." It's shocking to learn that in the United States a full quarter of the population believes in the "great replacement" theory (which contends that White people are being deliberately "replaced" through a secretive program by Black and Brown immigrants),[14, 15] or that 17 percent of Americans believe the government is controlled by "Satan-worshipping elites who run a child sex ring."[16]

When insecurity, distraction, and confusion reign, we burrow into a place of safety. Security is what psychologists call a classic "deficit value."[17, 18] Its importance escalates when we feel it is deficient, and we begin shutting out other values. This allows the very people who helped cause our insecurity to present themselves as our saviors, our "strongmen," to whom we can turn for refuge from the chaos they created. A survey by the Hansard Society revealed that 54 percent of respondents now agree with the statement "Britain needs a strong ruler willing to break the rules," whereas only 23 percent disagree.[19] A similar poll in the United States found that roughly 40 percent "tend to favor authority, obedience and uniformity over freedom, independence and diversity."[20] More strikingly, a 2022 poll revealed that 56 percent of Americans agreed with the sentiment that the "only way our country can get through the crisis ahead is to get back to our traditional values, put a tough leader in power, and silence the troublemakers spreading radical ideas."[21]

While we are mesmerized by imaginary threats, the power of the invisible doctrine continues to expand.

17.

CITIZENS OF
NOWHERE

The oligarch's interests lie offshore, in tax havens and secrecy regimes. Paradoxically, these interests are served
by politicians promoting a nationalist and nativist agenda.
The politicians who thunder about "patriotism," "sovereignty," and the "defense of our borders" are always the first
to sell their own countries down the river. It's no coincidence that the newspapers and television stations endlessly
fulminating about immigrants and sovereignty tend to be
owned by billionaire tax exiles living overseas.

As economic life has been offshored, so has political life.
The rules created to prevent foreign money from funding
domestic elections have, in large part, collapsed. Now, "action committees" and other aggregators of finance use shell
companies to hide the true sources of their funds.[1] Campaigns created by hidden interests—of which the work of
Cambridge Analytica (a company whose microtargeting of
voters with false claims about the European Union may
have helped to swing the small margin of the Brexit vote)[2]
is a prime example—spend dark money to mislead domestic electorates.

At the same time, power is drained from the nation state—its ability to collect taxes, defend workers, and regulate capital contracts. As the academics Reijer Hendrikse and Rodrigo Fernandez argue, offshore finance involves "the rampant unbundling and commercialization of state sovereignty,"[3] and the shifting of power into a secretive, extraterritorial legal space, beyond the control of any state. In this offshore world, they contend, "financialized and hypermobile global capital effectively *is* the state."

Globalization is not solely a neoliberal project, but it has been both shaped and accelerated by neoliberalism. Although political power has moved offshore, the means of holding it to account have not. Democracy stops at the national border, but the operations of the World Bank, the International Monetary Fund, the bodies regulating transnational trade, and the offshore arbitration systems circle the globe. As they have gained increasing power over the life of many nations, the interests of citizens—and the democratic means by which they can be heard—have been displaced by the "soft" form of "liberal dictatorship" that Hayek favored.

"Patriotic" politicians, such as the former British prime minister Theresa May, accuse those who care about the rights of people beyond national borders, as opposed to their own narrow domestic interests, of being "citizens of nowhere."[4] But the real citizens of nowhere are the billionaires who fund these "patriots." However far offshore such oligarchs travel, it is never far enough. Peter Thiel poured money into the Seasteading Institute,[5] founded by Milton

Friedman's grandson, which planned to build artificial islands in the middle of the ocean, where the very rich could escape from the constraints of taxation, regulation, trade unions, and all the other "encumbrances" they encountered.[6] But the ventures that the institute inspired sank after some of the investors began asking inconvenient questions: who will feed us, service our homes, clean our clothes, and supply the other goods and services we demand? Such is the force of the oligarchs' fantasy of detaching themselves from an ungrateful world that they managed to forget they are utterly dependent on the labor of others.

This pipe dream owes much to Ayn Rand's novels *Atlas Shrugged*[7] and *The Fountainhead*,[8] which are the fictional mirrors of *The Constitution of Liberty*, and the favorite texts of billionaires and teenage misanthropes. The Randian fantasy of a billionaires' strike against democratic controls, which would lead to the collapse of the world they order, teaching the ungrateful plebs to show some gratitude to their lords and masters, is a perfect inversion of reality. Working people don't need billionaires to run their lives, but the billionaires sure as hell need workers.

This far, and yet further. Scarcely a month now passes without a billionaire promoting their dream of setting up space pods or colonies on other planets. Governments amplify these delusions. NASA even runs a website devoted to the idea, claiming that gigantic spaceships "could be wonderful places to live; about the size of a California beach town and endowed with weightless recreation, fantastic views, freedom, elbow-room in spades, and great wealth."[9] Of course, no one could leave, except to enter another spaceship, and the slightest malfunction would result in annihilation. But "settlements in earth orbit will have one of the most stunning views in our solar system—the living, ever-changing Earth." As in Neil Blomkamp's dystopian sci-fi film *Elysium*, we can look back and remember wistfully how beautiful it was.

NASA's website continues by fantasizing about the money to be made. "Space colonization is, at its core, a real estate business. . . . Those that colonize space will control vast lands, enormous amounts of electrical power, and nearly unlimited material resources. [They] will create wealth beyond our wildest imagination and wield power—hopefully for good rather than for ill." Ah, yes, "hopefully." Hopefully, the colonization of this vast new *terra nullius* will be entirely different from the entire history of colonization on Earth. How and why?

A common characteristic of such fantasies is their lack of imagination. Wild flights of technological fancy are accompanied by a stolid incapacity to picture the inner life of these cosmic pioneers. Those who envisage human life on Earth ending because of power and greed and oppression somehow imagine we will escape these forces, while trapped in pressurized vessels controlled by technicians.

In these fantasies, we can detect the physical perpetuation of capitalism's ever-expanding frontier, in which it seeks both NASA's "vast lands, enormous amounts of electrical power, and nearly unlimited material resources," and to escape the consequences of its actions on Planet Earth. Never mind ecological collapse: "we" can flee to space stations or other planets . . . planets that have no eco-system at all. (Again, the "we" is carefully unspecified.)

The oligarchs' interests are endlessly conflicted. On the one hand, they are inextricably tied to the cheap labor on which their wealth depends, and the force and resources of the states that amplify their power. On the other, they are repelled by the social relations in which that labor and state power are embedded—the taxes and public protections, the collective bargaining, and the elections in which the poor are given a say in how things should work.

At the heart of neoliberalism is the fantasy of escape: escape from taxation and regulation, escape from the European Union and international law, escape from social obligation, escape from democracy. Escape, eventually, to a starlit wonderland beyond politics and beyond people.

18.

A FLAW IN THE MODEL

Perhaps the most important aspect of this story is also the least understood. One of the great deficiencies of our education is that few of us are taught complex systems theory. Yet everything of material importance to us—the human brain, the human body, human society, ecosystems, the atmosphere, the oceans, financial networks, economic structures—is a complex system.

We "learn" about these systems in school, but from the outset we are misled about their true nature. We are taught about complex systems as if they were linear, graduated, and simple. They are represented with flow diagrams, which are appropriate when applied to, say, plumbing or electrical circuits—but describe wholly different principles from those that govern complex systems.

All complex systems possess emergent properties. This means that their components, however simple they each might be, behave in nonlinear ways when they combine. Through networks created in ways that nobody could possibly have planned, via billions of randomly distributed decisions, they organize themselves—spontaneously creating order without central control.

Under certain conditions, a complex system will be resilient, as its self-organizing properties stabilize it. Under different conditions, these self-organizing properties can have the opposite effect. Negative feedback loops, which help keep systems stable, can be replaced by positive feedback loops, which compound the shocks afflicting the network, pushing it toward a critical threshold.

Even when it is close to this threshold, a system can appear stable to those who don't understand its dynamics. Instead of responding to stress in a linear and gradual way as a simple system might, it sustains its equilibrium state until the last minute, then collapses—suddenly and unstoppably. The factor that appears to cause the crash—like the US subprime crisis—can be tiny by comparison to the size of the system, and the stress much smaller than many others that it has weathered without ill effect. But the presenting cause is not necessarily the root cause. Small perturbations can tip over a system that, through years of erosion, has lost its resilience.

Having collapsed, a complex system quickly self-regulates to achieve a new equilibrium, which can be entirely different from the one that prevailed before, and hostile to those who depended on it. Its collapse cannot be easily reversed—if at all.[1]

Because so few of us study these systems, and there is no common understanding of how they operate, their behavior repeatedly takes us by surprise. The 2008 financial crash was a classic example. On visiting the London School of Economics in November of that year, Queen Elizabeth II asked the question on everyone's lips: "Why did nobody notice it?"[2] In other words, why didn't anyone see the crash coming? The eminent professors in attendance cleared their throats and studied their feet.

The economist who would later produce what seems to be the most coherent answer to the Queen's question was Andy Haldane, then an executive at the Bank of England. In the hope of grasping the underlying reasons for the crisis that took almost everyone by surprise, he made an inspired choice. He approached one of the pioneers of systems theory, the ecologist Robert May. They eventually published their findings in *Nature*, in a joint paper called "Systemic Risk in Banking Ecosystems."[3] In a speech to the Bank of England,[4] Haldane summarized what he had learned.

Finance, he explained, is a complex adaptive system, like a rainforest or a marine food web. The diversity of this system had been steadily eroded prior to the 2008 crash, as every financial institution pursued broadly the same, increasingly complex strategy. Paradoxically, they called their convergent approaches "diversification strategies." Each bank appeared to spread the risk it was taking, by developing new, ever more exotic and opaque products.

"Risk became a commodity" that was "bundled, sliced, diced and then re-bundled for onward sale," in a system that had been dangerously deregulated. But because their underlying strategies were similar, financial institutions actually concentrated the risk across the system as a whole. In other words, while the firms each became internally more diverse, the system as a whole became less diverse. Diversity is a key component of systemic resilience.

The banks also became more strongly connected to one another, reinforcing the synchronization of their behavior. As Haldane pointed out, up to a certain point, connections absorb shocks within a complex system. Beyond a certain degree of connectivity, however, they amplify these shocks—and "the system acts not as a mutual insurance device but as a mutual incendiary device." At that point, a small shock—like the American subprime crisis—can tip it into collapse (a collapse, in this case, narrowly averted by the massive global bank bailout).

This problem was exacerbated by the growth of the network's key "nodes"—the banks that had merged and expanded after Bill Clinton's repeal in 1999 of the 1933 Glass-Steagall Act—and the way they became focal points for the entire financial system. Having what Haldane called a "small number of financial hubs with multiple spokes" is part of the recipe for systemic disaster.

A crucial feature of neoliberal thought is the belief that what is good for one is good for all. Ignoring Adam Smith's many warnings about human self-interest and fallibility, neoliberals created a mantra out of a single, decontextualized phrase of his: that the "invisible hand" of private interest will "advance the interest of society, and afford means to the multiplication of the species."[5] What systems theory reveals is that this "invisible hand" can have the opposite effect.

When the banks were deregulated—in line with neoliberal theory—the policy was supported by Democrats and Republicans, Labour and the Conservatives alike. Neoliberal theorists claimed that by pulling down the walls between banking institutions and the regulatory firebreaks that restrained their behavior, by allowing them to pursue whatever outlandish strategies appeared to advance their individual interests, by letting the biggest of them grow as much as they wished, allowing them to swallow their competitors and dominate the system, the system as a whole would gain in strength—what was good for one was good for all. But as Haldane, drawing on systems science, explained, while every decision might seem economically rational for the bank that takes it, the unrestrained pursuit of apparent self-interest can make the system less resilient. The individual interest and the collective interest are not the same.

The 2008 financial crisis was a clear and indisputable refutation of both neoliberal theory and neoliberal practice. Even Alan Greenspan, the chair of the US Federal Reserve, who had literally sat at Ayn Rand's knee[6] (he was a devoted member of her inner circle, founder-member of the Ayn Rand Collective, and adherent of her "objectivist" philosophy, which has much in common with neoliberalism, though it is even more extreme), found himself obliged to concede his "mistake." What was this mistake? To believe that, by operating in their own self-interest, the banks would act in the interests of all. There was, he admitted, "a flaw in the model . . . that defines how the world works."[7]

This must stand as one of the understatements of the decade. What the crisis exposed was not only specific and individual flaws in the model, but the erroneous belief that a system tailored to suit those with the most rapacious tendencies will supernaturally lead to widespread prosperity.

But even a global crisis that came perilously close to tanking the world economy wasn't enough to dissuade the believers and beneficiaries of neoliberalism. The most remarkable aspect of this saga is the way in which the Neoliberal International picked itself up, explained the crisis away, and carried on, promoting the same flawed model of how the world works—as if nothing had changed. The media and the governments they either owned or influenced were, of course, fully complicit in this gaslighting.

Today, neoliberal governments seek yet again to roll back the regulations that were hastily reimposed on the banks in the wake of the crisis. Inexorably, deregulation leads to dysfunction: banks fail, offshore oil rigs spill, airlines go bankrupt, trains derail, and the Earth burns. Despite the crushing refutation of the ideology in 2008, neoliberalism continues to dominate our lives.

19.
NO EXIT

But perhaps the greatest of all neoliberal "market failures" transcends balance sheets, growth reports, and quarterly dividends. It concerns another set of complex systems: those on which all our lives depend. Earth systems also respond to stress in nonlinear ways—they, too, have tipping points.

From inception, if we accept Madeira's sugar plantations as the first case that fully meets our definition, capitalism has been a frenetic assault on the living planet. The charred wastes left in its wake are as intrinsic to capitalism as the commodification of labor.

The effect of neoliberal globalization has been to turn the Earth into a single island, an island that can be traversed by capital in a second. As the fire-front unceasingly rolls across the globe, it finds ever less to burn, so it works its way down what could be described as the entropic food chain.

You can see this most clearly in the exploitation of natural resources: the richest and most accessible are taken first. The global fishing fleet takes out the large predators—bluefin tuna, Patagonian toothfish, halibut—then, when those have been exhausted, it targets ever smaller species, until all that's left is the process of mopping up baitfish. These, in an attempt to push the operation back up the value chain, are then fed to farmed predators, such as salmon. Loggers in tropical forests took the mahogany, the rosewood, and the pau brasil first, then went back for less valuable fine-timber species, before returning with ply and pulp mills to process what remained. Oil companies, upon depleting the most accessible oilfields, turn to the tar sands, oil shale, the ocean floor, and the Arctic for extraction—employing ever more costly, inefficient, and environmentally destructive methods.

Capitalism's genius is expressed in its ability to develop ever more inventive and aggressive strategies for extracting diminishing human and planetary resources. But eventually the fire-front must run out of fuel.

Globalization, from this perspective, is an extension of colonial looting. What looked like the beginning of an era of permanent global prosperity now looks more like a period of extreme exploitation and consumption that simply cannot be sustained or repeated. Just as the slaves on Madeira had to be sent ever farther afield to find the *madeira* (wood) on which the sugar industry depended, reducing the operation's productivity, so capital must now work the planet's people and resources ever harder, to extract diminishing returns. This might help to explain the inability of governments almost everywhere, despite their extreme and often highly damaging efforts, to recover the levels of growth they once achieved.

In the end, all the world is Madeira.

Capitalism is not the only economic system to have scorched and poisoned the planet. Soviet and Chinese Communism have also caused spectacular environmental disasters. But capitalism is the system deemed by its champions to have triumphed. It is the system that has been universalized across the planet (albeit with regional variations), with catastrophic environmental consequences. So this is the system we need to address. And neoliberalism, as we have seen, is its accelerant.

For neoliberals, the consumption of the living world is not just collateral damage, but something approaching a sacred duty. This is what Hayek wrote in *The Constitution of Liberty*:

> It is the belief [of conservationists] that the natural fertility of the soil should in all circumstances be preserved and that what is branded as "soil mining" should in all circumstances be avoided. It can be easily shown that as a general proposition, this is unsound . . . In fact, "soil mining" may in certain circumstances be as much in the long-range interests of the community as the using-up of any stock resource. . . . [In these circumstances] it will be desirable to allow the fertility to decline to the level at which investments will still pay. . . . To use up a free gift of nature once and for all is in such instances no more wasteful or reprehensible than a similar exploitation of a stock resource.[1]

In other words, as long as there is economic gain in converting nature into money, we should do so.

But we depend on this "stock resource"—the soil—for 99 percent of our calories.[2] Thanks to soil mining, we exploit and exhaust it faster than it can regenerate. In some of the world's most food-stressed nations, more than 70 percent of the arable land is now suffering severe degradation.[3]

Soil damage in dry places is one of the reasons why the growth in grain yields in sub-Saharan Africa has been so weak over the past sixty years,[4] while they have boomed in the rest of the world. Even in the rich temperate nations, where the weather is milder (and therefore inflicts less damage on exposed soil), and people are not forced by poverty to cultivate steep slopes, depletion rates severely threaten food security. Governments were able, as if by magic, to forestall financial collapse in 2008 by conjuring up future money: a process they called "quantitative easing," in which a central bank buys up government bonds to stimulate the economy and increase the money supply. But you cannot prevent the collapse of our food system by conjuring up future food.

Neoliberal globalization seeks to outsource pollution to places where political resistance is weakest: kleptocracies in the poor world and communities desperate for jobs are used as dumping grounds for everything from tires to fast fashion to hospital waste. They are removed from the sight and minds of people conditioned to buy the shiny new products that fuel consumer-led growth. But, as we now know, some pollutants—regardless of where they are dumped—have global impacts. Among these "externalities"—the bureaucratic, neutral-sounding term used by economists—is carbon dioxide, which does not disperse but accumulates in the atmosphere. Partly because most rich nations are temperate, and partly because of the extreme poverty in former colonies, resulting from centuries of looting, the effects of carbon dioxide and other greenhouse gases are, like other impacts of capitalism, felt most by those who have benefited the least from their production.

The wealthy nations, always keen to position themselves as saviors, have promised to help their former colonies adjust to the chaos they have caused. Since 2009, rich countries have pledged $100 billion a year to poorer ones in the form of climate finance.[5] Unsurprisingly, delivery has fallen far short of this promise.[6] But even if the money had materialized, it would have been a mere token. By comparison, since 2015, the G20 nations have spent $3.3 trillion on subsidizing their fossil-fuel industries.[7]

Instead, the richest nations have poured money into keeping out the people fleeing from climate breakdown and other disasters. Between 2013 and 2018, the United Kingdom spent almost twice as much on sealing its borders as it did on climate finance.[8] The United States spent eleven times, Australia thirteen times, and Canada fifteen times more. Collectively, the rich nations are fortifying themselves with a rampart to exclude the victims of their own waste products. Already, the manufactured hatred of refugees has helped the far right to gain or share power in Italy, Sweden, and Hungary, and has greatly enhanced its prospects in the Netherlands, Spain, Austria, France, and even Germany. As these parties, backed as they always are by oligarchs and corporations, tend to crush environmental protections, their electoral gains accelerate the ecological collapse driving people from their homes, leading in turn to greater opportunities for the far right.[9]

The power accumulated by fossil-fuel companies through fifty years of plunder has enabled them to make stupendous profits, a staggering $2.8 billion a day on average across that period.[10] They need invest only a fraction of these profits to buy sufficient politicians, policies, and, in some cases, entire political systems, to prevent the replacement of our fossil-based systems with less damaging alternatives.

You can bargain with politics. You can bargain with economics. But you cannot bargain with physics. To secure just a 50 percent chance (not great odds, considering what's at stake)[11] of preventing 2.7°F of global heating, current estimates suggest that almost 60 percent of the remaining oil and fossil gas reserves must be left in the ground.[12] In short, that means no new fossil-fuel development. If we want a higher chance of averting planetary disaster, almost all fossil fuels—including those fields already in production—need to remain unexploited.[13] The countries that have the greatest capacity to invest in alternative sources of energy need to lead the way. But the tremendous lobbying power of the fossil-fuel industry prevents this outcome. In the UK, for example, the government hands back 91 pence of every pound it harvests in the form of the Energy Profits Levy (a form of tax) to oil and gas companies drilling for new sources.[14]

We no longer need to speculate about where this path

might lead—many parts of the world are already experiencing the hard realities. In 2022, floods in Pakistan displaced 33 million people and washed away 3 million acres of soil.[15] The floods were followed by a crop-shriveling heatwave. This is the "whipsaw effect" predicted in scientific papers:[16] moderate weather gives way to a violent cycle of extremes. It's hard to see how the country will ever recover from the economic and agricultural shocks of these disasters: just as Pakistan begins to pick itself up, it's likely to be knocked down by another crisis.

India, Nigeria, Indonesia, the Philippines, Afghanistan, Papua New Guinea, Sudan, Niger, Burkina Faso, Mali, and Central America also face extreme risks.[17] Weather events such as massive floods and intensified cyclones and hurricanes will keep hammering countries such as Pakistan, Mozambique, Zimbabwe, Haiti, and Myanmar. Many people will have to move or die. Current global policies are likely to result in about 4.9°F of global heating by 2100. On this trajectory, scientific modeling has forecast that some 2 billion people may be stranded in inhospitable conditions by global heating by 2030, and 3.7 billion by 2090.[18] These figures do not take into account the effect of rising sea levels, which could displace hundreds of millions more.

In 2022, though sparsely reported in the Western media, China suffered the greatest heat anomaly ever recorded anywhere on Earth.[19] Wildfires roared across Siberia and Alaska—in many cases, searing deep into peat soils and releasing plumes of carbon dioxide and methane that, in turn, cause even more global heating. Torrents of meltwater poured from the Greenland ice cap, sweltering under a 14.4°F temperature anomaly.[20] In 2023, smoke from raging Canadian wildfires descended upon major American cities, temporarily inflicting the worst air quality in the world (ironically coinciding with Canada's national Clean Air Day).[21, 22] Seawater off the coast of Florida reached the temperature—101°F, or 38°C—of a hot shower.[23] Heatwaves in parts of Asia and the American southwest are reaching the point at which the human body hits its thermal limits. Ever-wider swathes of the world will come to rely on air-conditioning for human survival—yet another feedback spiral, as air-conditioning increases energy use.

A devastating four-year drought in the Horn of Africa between 2018 and 2022 offers a glimpse of what "uninhabitable" may look like.[24] As large tracts of the world lose their ability to support human life, those who can afford it will move—those who cannot will die. But, to some neoliberal thinkers, this is simply the price of progress.

The neoliberal economist Andrew Lilico is one among many proposing that humanity will just have to live with climate breakdown, as we "can't afford" to stop it happening. He wrote a column for the *Daily Telegraph* titled "We Have Failed to Prevent Global Warming, So We Must Adapt to It."[25]

Once again, the two uses of "we" in this headline referred to different people. "We, the owners of fossil-fuel plants or the profits that arise from them" can accept no new taxation to encourage green energy or regulation to discourage the consumption of fossil fuels. This "we" cannot adapt even to the slightest interruption of the profit pipeline. But the other "we," which turns out to mean "they"—the countless millions of people in the Global South—can and must adapt to the loss of their homes, their land, and their lives. When challenged on Twitter to explain how people in the tropics might adapt to a world in which 4°C (around 7°F) of global warming had happened, Lilico replied:

> I imagine tropics adapt to 4C world by being wastelands with few folk living in them. Why's that not an option?[26]

Such psychopathic reasoning points to a common characteristic of neoliberal thought: everything is mutable, except neoliberal economic theory. Billions can be driven from their homes or left to starve, the ecology and society of entire tracts of the planet can be allowed to collapse, but nothing can be permitted to interfere with what neoliberals present as the "natural laws" of neoliberal economics. Once we transform all of the living world into money, the invisible hand will somehow ensure that our material needs are met. While the planet is regarded as disposable as a paper coffee cup, the ideology causing this destruction cannot be contested.

Our predicament—the greatest humanity has ever faced—is often characterized as a climate crisis. But it would be more accurate to call it an Earth systems crisis. Soil degradation, freshwater depletion, marine ecological collapse, habitat destruction, species extinction, and the impact of pesticides and other synthetic chemicals—each of these factors may be comparable in scale and effect to climate breakdown. What we are witnessing is the breakdown, at astonishing speed, of our life-support systems—driven by capitalism, accelerated by neoliberalism.

20.

THE MICRO-SOLUTIONS MYTH

Neoliberalism's flawed model of how the world works leads to similar outcomes in every sphere of activity: finance, human prosperity, mental health, ecosystems. To admit anything is to admit everything. So, instead of addressing these flaws, corporate and oligarchic capital seeks to disguise them.

One means of doing so has been to shift responsibility from government and structural forces to individual forces, blaming ordinary people for the very crises that have been imposed on them. Just as the poor have been condemned for their poverty—and sometimes come to internalize this belief—so "consumers" have been blamed for the economic model driving the Sixth Great Extinction of life on Earth.

This shift from addressing our problems collectively to addressing them individually points to what is arguably the most decisive transition in communications strategy of the past fifty years. In a brilliant public-relations coup, we have been induced by corporate marketing and media propaganda to ignore massive economic and political forces, and focus instead on individual micro-solutions. Through yet another counterintuitive hustle, consumerism—the presenting problem—is also presented as the answer. We are inculcated with the belief that we don't need to stop consuming—in fact, we need to *keep* consuming, just "consume better."

The conscious effort to stop us from seeing the bigger picture began in 1953, with a campaign called "Keep America Beautiful."[1] Its most famous product was a 1970 television advertisement featuring a "Native American" (who turned out to be an Italian) standing beside a littered highway with a single, noble tear running down his cheek. Keep America Beautiful was pure Astroturf. It looked as if it were created by environmental activists, but it was devised and funded by packaging manufacturers, including Coca-Cola. They were seeking to shift responsibility for the tsunami of disposable plastic packaging they'd created and to sink state laws ensuring that glass bottles were returned and reused. Keep America Beautiful invented the term "litterbugs." The story it told was that irresponsible, antisocial consumers were at fault rather than the corporations that had dumped a massive problem—single-use, nondegradable packaging—onto a system ill equipped to deal with it.

Four decades later, the "Love Where You Live" campaign, launched in the UK in 2011 by Keep Britain Tidy—in partnership with Imperial Tobacco and the American multinationals McDonald's and the candy and chewing-gum manufacturer Wrigley—appeared to play a similar role.[2] The program was "built on principles that include encouraging personal responsibility," by way of mobilizing volunteers to handle many of the services the state had cut (or sought to cut further)—including trash removal and cleaning up the streets, beaches, and waterways in their communities. It had the added bonus—as it featured strongly in classrooms—of granting Imperial Tobacco exposure to schoolchildren: its corporate logo was juxtaposed with the campaign's green heart symbol in materials distributed to schools and other public bodies.[3]

One of the most damaging and effective channels for this blame-shifting was established in 2004, when the advertising company Ogilvy & Mather, working for the oil giant BP, championed the idea of the "personal carbon footprint."[4] This was, in some ways, a useful innovation, but it also had the effect of diverting political pressure away from the producers of fossil fuels and toward consumers. The oil industry's hypocrisy apparently knows no bounds. In 2019, Shell Oil's chief executive, Ben van Beurden, gave a speech instructing us to "eat seasonally and recycle more."[5] He publicly berated his chauffeur for buying strawberries in January, imported from overseas with the use of fossil fuels (who, we might ask, supplied them?). In 2022, civil proceedings were brought against van Beurden and twelve other Shell executives for ignoring a Dutch court ruling to reduce its carbon emissions.[6, 7] (While van Beurden would ultimately resign in the fallout, Shell's army of lawyers continues to appeal the court's decision.)

Too often, we focus on tiny issues such as plastic straws and coffee cups rather than the huge structural forces—the power of corporate lobbyists and the money they wield—driving us toward catastrophe. We're obsessed with plastic bags. We believe we're doing the world a favor by buying tote bags instead—although, according to one estimate, the environmental impact of producing an organic cotton tote bag is equivalent to that of 20,000 plastic ones.[8]

The public has been intentionally misled about the efficacy of recycling because, in the words of one industry insider, "If the public thinks that recycling is working, then they're not going to be as concerned about the environment."[9] For decades now, plastic-recycling campaigns have been promoted and funded by Big Oil and plastics manufacturers like Exxon, Chevron, Dow, and DuPont, which have pushed for legislation that would mandate the "international recycling symbol" (you know, the triangle of arrows) to be stamped on *all* plastics—even those that can't be economically recycled—in the full knowledge that broad-scale recycling was both "costly" and "unlikely."[10] In the words of one investigative reporter, "We found that the industry sold the public on an idea it knew wouldn't work—that the majority of plastic could be, and would be, recycled—all while making billions of dollars selling the world new plastic." As the demand for oil for vehicles is likely to decline, plastic production accounts for $400 billion a year in offsetting revenue—an amount expected to triple by 2050,[11] securing the oil industry's survival.

There are some meaningful actions we can take as consumers: primarily, traveling less and differently (especially by ceasing to fly), and switching to a plant-based diet. But in most other sectors, it scarcely matters how green you think you are. Studies of "green" and "nongreen" consumers show that the main driver of a person's environmental impact is not their attitude. It is not their mode of consumption or the particular choices they make.[12] It's their money.[13] If people have surplus money, they spend it. While you might persuade yourself that you are a green mega-consumer, in reality you are just a mega-consumer. This is why the environmental impacts of the very rich, however eco-friendly they may appear to be, are massively greater than those of everyone else.[14]

Preventing more than 1.5°C of global heating means that our average emissions should be no greater than two tons of carbon dioxide, per person, per year.[15] But the richest 1 percent of the world's people produce an average of more than 70 tons annually.[16] Together, they release 15 percent of the world's carbon emissions: twice the combined impact of the poorest half of the world's population. Bill Gates, according to one estimate, emits almost 7,500 tons of CO_2 per year, mostly from flying in his private jets and helicopters.[17] Roman Abramovich, the same figures suggest, produces almost 34,000 tons, largely by running his gigantic yachts (he currently owns sixteen, collectively worth more than $2 billion).[18]

The multiple homes owned by ultra-rich people might be fitted with solar panels, their supercars might be electric, their private planes might run on biokerosene—but these tweaks make little difference to the overall impact of their consumption. In some cases they increase it. The switch to biofuels favored by Bill Gates is now among the greatest causes of habitat destruction, as forests are felled to produce wood pellets and liquid fuels, and soils are trashed to make biomethane.[19]

But more important than the direct impacts of the

ultra-wealthy is the political and cultural power with which they block effective change. Their cultural power relies on yet another hypnotizing fairy tale.

Capitalism persuades us that we are all temporarily embarrassed millionaires. This is why we tolerate it. In reality, some people are extremely rich because others are extremely poor: massive wealth depends on exploitation. If we did all become millionaires, we'd cook the planet to a crisp in no time at all. But the fairy tale of universal wealth "one day" secures our obedience. In consenting to the continued destruction of our life-support systems, in the hope that one day we might also number among the winners, we internalize, yet again, capitalism's justifying stories.

In 1947, in the wake of the development and use of the atomic bomb, the Bulletin of Atomic Scientists created a mechanism called the Doomsday Clock to warn the public how close we are to destroying our world. It was originally set at seven minutes to midnight. At the time of this writing—taking nuclear risk, climate change, biological threats, and disruptive technologies into consideration—the clock stands at ninety seconds to midnight, the closest to global catastrophe it has ever been. We can't afford to throw away our future for a fairy tale.

21.

MOBILIZATION: A CASE STUDY

No part of the neoliberal program can succeed without the stifling of hope. One of the most powerful aspects of neoliberalism is the hopelessness it induces by persuading us that "there is no alternative"—a phrase Margaret Thatcher used so often that it was condensed to an acronym, "TINA." By presenting this extreme doctrine as if it were nothing but a description of the natural order—the way things are and have to be—the Neoliberal International persuaded many of us that no other strategy was possible.

"There's no money." "It would interrupt growth." "The people wouldn't stand for it." Governments repeatedly seek to persuade us that they are incapable of action, unable to govern, that their hands are tied, that their uselessness is baked in. They can't address poverty. They can't ensure that the elderly, or the sick, or the addicted are properly looked after. They can't prevent the collapse of roads, bridges, or school buildings, let alone of ecosystems. It's all beyond their control. Instead, they teach us to be hopeless and to expect no relief—accelerating the diseases of despair, the eco-anxiety, the nihilism, and the apathy to which so many people understandably succumb.

But governments have repeatedly proven to be capable of decisive action—when they choose to be or when circumstance forces their hand. Whenever the "free market" has stumbled, government has intervened without hesitation, spending whatever it takes to rescue neoliberalism from its own disasters. Examples include bailing out Chrysler in 1980, the airline industry bailout in 2001, the savings and loan crisis of 1989, and the financial crisis of 2008. During the Covid-19 pandemic, money that states had sworn they didn't have suddenly and magically materialized. Governments discovered they could govern (albeit with varying degrees of competence). People turned out to be prepared, when they felt they were contributing to the common good, to change their behavior radically.

But the problems we face today require even more ambitious intervention: a fair, prosperous, sustainable society cannot materialize under current conditions. We need a radical transformation. Impossible? Let's take a look at what happened when the United States joined the Second World War.

Before the US declared war, President Franklin Roosevelt had begun to draft troops and build his "arsenal of democracy": the materiel with which he supplied the Allied forces. To "outbuild Hitler," he called for levels of production previously considered impossible. But, following the Japanese attack on Pearl Harbor on December 7, 1941, the impossible was turned—through sheer force of will—into reality.

The day after the attack, Roosevelt requested a declaration of war from Congress. Once it was in hand, he immediately set to work reorganizing not only the government but the entire nation. He launched a series of agencies that were overseen and coordinated through simple but effective measures, such as the Controlled Materials Plan (CMP)—a system of quotas, priorities, and restrictions on the use of materials to ensure efficient production and resource allocation.[1]

The president introduced, for the first time in US history, general federal income taxes. The government rapidly raised the top rate until, in 1944, it reached 94 percent.[2] It issued war bonds. It borrowed massively. Between 1940 and 1945, total government spending rose roughly *tenfold*. Astonishingly, the US government spent more money (in current dollar terms) between 1942 and 1945 than it had between 1789 and 1941.[3] From 1940 to 1944, its military budget rose by a factor of forty-two, outstripping the budgets of Germany, Japan, and the United Kingdom put together.

Civilian industries in the United States were entirely retooled for war. When the car industry was instructed to switch to military production, its massive equipment was swiftly jackhammered out of the floor and replaced, often in a matter of weeks, with new machines.[4] General Motors began turning out tanks, aircraft engines, fighter planes, cannons, and machine guns.[5] Oldsmobile started making artillery shells; Pontiac produced antiaircraft guns. By 1944, Ford was building a long-range bomber plane almost every hour.[6] During its three years of war, the United

States manufactured 87,000 naval vessels, including 27 aircraft carriers; 300,000 planes; 100,000 tanks and armored cars; and 44 billion rounds of ammunition.[7] Roosevelt described it as a "miracle of production." But it wasn't a miracle. It was the realization of a well-laid plan.

The US war effort mobilized tens of millions of people. Between 1940 and the end of the war, the number of American troops rose twenty-sixfold,[8] while the civilian labor force increased by ten million. Many of the new workers were women.

From 1942 until 1945 the manufacture of cars was banned.[9] So were new household appliances and even the construction of new homes. Tires and gasoline were strictly rationed; meat, butter, sugar, clothes, and shoes were also limited. Rationing was considered fairer than taxing scarce goods: it ensured that everyone received an equal share. A national speed limit of 35mph was imposed, to save fuel.

Posters warned people: "When you ride ALONE, you ride with Hitler! Join a car-sharing club TODAY,"[10] and asked: "Is this trip really necessary?"[11] They cautioned: "Waste helps the enemy: conserve material." Americans were urged to sign the Consumer's Victory Pledge: "I will buy carefully; I will take good care of the things I have; I will waste nothing."[12] Every imaginable material—chewing-gum wrappers, rubber bands, used cooking fat—was recycled.

So what stops the world from responding with the same decisive force to the greatest crisis humanity has ever faced? It's not a lack of money, or capacity, or technology (if anything, digitization would make transformation quicker and easier). It's the political thinking that persuades us such shifts are impossible. It's political will.

Catastrophe is not a matter of fate. It's a matter of choice. Our inability to respond to our current crises as the United States did more than eighty years ago is a stark illustration of a general rule: Political failure, at heart, is a failure of imagination.

We need a new story.

22.

A NEW STORY

To grapple with neoliberalism, you must first recognize and appreciate its genius: a collective genius, produced by its army of academics, economists, intellectuals, social psychologists, and public-relations experts—all bought and paid for, refining and packaging the doctrine for public consumption. There is a kind of brilliance in its transformation of the deeply unpopular musings of a handful of eccentric economists into the dominant story of our lives.

Stories are the means by which we navigate the world. They allow us to interpret its complex and contradictory signals. They create meaning out of chaos.

When we want to make sense of something, the sense we seek is not scientific sense, but narrative fidelity. Does what we're hearing reflect the way we expect the world to behave? Does it hang together? Does it progress as a story should? Does it feel satisfying?

We are creatures of narrative. Facts and figures, essential as they are, cannot dislodge a persuasive story. You can't take away someone's story without giving them a new one. The only thing that can replace a story—is a story.

If a story is to make narrative sense to us, it needs a

structure. There are a number of basic plots that we find intuitively satisfying: narrative structures that have been used repeatedly, because they resonate with our attempts to find meaning. In politics there is a basic plot that is used again and again, because of its tremendous narrative power. We call it "the Restoration Story." It goes as follows:

> Disorder afflicts the land, caused by powerful and nefarious forces working against the interests of humanity. But the hero or heroes will rise up and revolt against this disorder, do battle with those powerful forces and, against all odds, emerge victorious to restore harmony to the land.

This is a familiar narrative structure. It's the plot we follow in the New Testament, in the Harry Potter books, in the Lord of the Rings books, in the Narnia books. It's also the story that has accompanied almost every political and religious transformation across millennia. We could go so far as to say that, without a powerful new restoration story, political and religious transformation would not be possible.

After laissez-faire economics triggered the Great Depression, John Maynard Keynes devised a new economics. But he did more than that. He told a new restoration story. It went like this.

> Disorder afflicts the land, caused by the powerful and nefarious forces of the economic elite, who have captured the world's wealth. But the hero of the story,

the enabling state, supported by working and middle-class people, will contest this disorder. It will fight those powerful forces by redistributing wealth and, through spending public money on public goods and services, will generate income and jobs, restoring harmony to the land.

Like all good restoration stories, this one resonated across the political spectrum. Democrats and Republicans, Labour and Conservatives, left and right all became, in broad terms, Keynesian. It was only when Keynesianism ran into trouble in the 1970s that the neoliberals were able to come forward with their own restoration story, which by then had been honed and polished for three decades. Remember what Milton Friedman said: "When the time came, we were ready . . . and we could step straight in." It went as follows:

Disorder afflicts the land, caused by the powerful and nefarious forces of an overbearing and over-reaching state, whose collectivizing tendencies have crushed freedom, individualism and opportunity. But the hero of the story, the freedom-seeking entrepreneur, will fight those powerful forces. He will roll back the paralyzing restrictions of the state and, through creating wealth and opportunity that will trickle down to all, restore harmony to the land.

This story also resonated across the political spectrum. Republicans and Democrats, Conservatives and Labour all became, in broad terms, neoliberal. Keynesianism and neo-liberalism were, more or less, opposite stories. Nonetheless, they used an identical narrative structure.

Then, in 2008, the neoliberal story imploded. It was at this moment that those of us who had suffered and con-tested its impacts across so many years discovered two things. First, that neoliberalism didn't work, even on its own terms. Second, that throughout this period we had failed to develop a new and resonant political story of our own. The best we had to offer was either a watered-down version of neoliberalism or a microwaved Keynesianism.

This, above all other factors, is why neoliberalism—despite all its failures—continues to dominate our lives: We have produced no new story with which to replace it. In politics, with one exception, you cannot go backward. That exception is fascism, whose grim story (also a restora-tion story, by the way, "The world has been thrown into disorder by a cosmopolitan elite, etc., etc. . . ."), manages to find new traction with each generation, particularly when social and economic conditions break down. But with this exception, people seem resistant to the retelling of an old political story. To capture the political imagination, we need a new one.

When we have no story that explains the present or describes the future, hope evaporates. Without a restora-tion story that can show us a way forward, nothing can change. With such a restoration story, almost everything can. The story we need to tell is one that will appeal to as wide a range of people as possible, crossing political fault lines. It should resonate with deep needs and desires. It should be simple and intelligible, and it should be grounded in reality.

This might sound like a tall order, but we believe such a story exists and is waiting to be told.

Over the past few years, findings from several different sciences—psychology, anthropology, neuroscience, evolutionary biology—have pointed to something that should be obvious, and would be, had we not been induced to believe the Hobbesian notion that competition is the default state of humanity. As it turns out, we have a remarkable capacity for altruism.[1] While we all possess some degree of selfishness and greed, these are not our dominant values.[2] Most people are primarily motivated by more social values: altruism, empathy, family, community, and the pursuit of a better world—not only for themselves but also for others.

We are also, among mammals, the supreme cooperators, able to work together toward common ends in far more complex and preemptive ways than other mammals can. These are the central, crucial characteristics of humankind: our astonishing altruism and cooperation. But something has gone horribly wrong.

Our good nature has been thwarted by several forces—not least of which is the dominant political narrative of our times, one that motivates us to live in competition with one another. It encourages conflict, drives us to fear and mistrust one another. It atomizes society. It weakens the social bonds that make our lives worth living. In this vacuum, violent and intolerant forces grow.

But it doesn't have to be like this. We can recover the best attributes of our humanity: our altruism and cooperation. Where there is atomization, we can build a thriving civic life with a rich participatory culture. Where we find ourselves crushed between market and state, we can build an economics that respects both people and planet.

Where we have been ignored and exploited, we can revive our politics. We can recover democracy from the people who have captured it. We can use new, fairer election rules to ensure that financial power never trumps democratic power again. Representative democracy should be tempered by participatory democracy, enabling us to refine our political choices. These choices should be exercised as much as possible at the local level. If something can be decided locally, it should not be determined nationally.

We call this shift, which aims to reclaim some of the powers that have been taken from our communities, the "politics of belonging"—something we believe can appeal to a wide range of people. Among the few values shared by both the left and the right are belonging and community. We might mean slightly different things by them, but at least we can begin with a common language. A large part of politics can be seen as a search for belonging—a fundamental human need. Even fascists seek community and belonging, albeit a disturbing version where everyone looks the same, believes the same, wears the same uniform, waves the same flag, and chants the same slogans.

Steering people away from fascism—a common response to political and societal dysfunction—requires an answer to the need for belonging. Fascism seeks a *bonding network*: one that brings together people from a homogeneous group. Its antithesis is the *bridging network*: one that brings together people from different groups. Only through building sufficiently rich and vibrant bridging communities can we hope to thwart people's urge to burrow into the security of a bonding community, defending themselves against the "other."

So our new restoration story could go something like this:

Disorder afflicts the land, caused by the powerful and nefarious forces of people who tell us that our highest purpose in life is to fight like stray dogs over a garbage can. But the heroes of the story, the common people long deprived of the democratic power we were promised, will revolt against this disorder. We will fight those nefarious forces by building rich, engaging, collaborative, inclusive, and generous communities. In doing so, we will restore harmony to the land.

Our task is to tell the story that will light the path to a better world.

23.

THE POLITICS OF BELONGING

Nothing in politics is permanent, no victory is definitive, nor should it be. Political life can be seen as a perpetual struggle against oppressive power. In neoliberalism, the very rich found an argument that justified their own oppressive power and then hired the best minds they could buy to refine their narrative into a powerful and resilient doctrine.

When neoliberalism is challenged or replaced by a new political story, those who wish to extend their power at the expense of others will endeavor to find another means of persuading us that what is good for them is good for everyone. Then another. And another. The moment when society stops seeking new means of confronting the constant innovation of the elites is the moment when politics fails.

We have a disadvantage in that we will never attract the kind of money on which the Neoliberal International can draw. But we have an advantage in that we can speak directly to—rather than against—the interests of the great majority of people.

We need to restore social meaning to terms that have been captured and coopted by the very forces against whom they were originally aimed. Terms such as "liberty," "taking back control," and "elite power."

By "liberty," we mean not the freedom of the very rich to do whatever they please, regardless of the consequences, but broad-based and widely shared freedoms. This requires us to place democratic restraints on oppressive, monopolistic, and destructive forms of power. By "taking back control," we mean enabling people to determine the political and economic course of their lives, in ways that do not limit other people's self-determination. By "elite power," we mean the power of those who exercise real economic and political dominance rather than anyone with a college education.

But how do we pursue these values without creating new systems of oppression? How do we, after decades of the disenchantment of politics by economics, re-enchant politics?

One of the strangest, most counterintuitive aspects of modern political life is the acceptance, in supposedly democratic societies, of behaviors we wouldn't tolerate in any other context. In many societies, controlling and coercive behavior in relationships is no longer legal. But when politicians treat us this way, we celebrate them as "strong leaders."

In the dominant model of representative democracy, hundreds of issues are bundled together at every election, yet the vote tends to swing on just one or two of them. The government then presumes consent for its entire policy platform and, if it commands a majority in Congress or Parliament, for anything else it wants to introduce. We don't accept presumed consent in sex. Why should we accept it in politics?

A common riposte to anyone who seeks political change is "So why don't you run for office?" This suggests that the only valid political role a citizen can play is to become a representative, and that between elections only the elected few have a legitimate voice. This is democracy in the shallowest and weakest sense—an open invitation for the capture of a system by elites. But much richer conceptions of democracy have been proposed.

One such model has been described by the late Murray Bookchin, an American foundryman, autoworker, and shop steward who became a professor in the field he helped to develop: social ecology. In his book *The Next Revolution*,[1] he makes a crucial distinction between *statecraft* and *politics*. He sees the state as a force for domination, and statecraft as the means by which it is sustained. Politics, by contrast, is "the active engagement of free citizens" in their own affairs. He sees the municipality (village, town, or city) as the place in which we first began to explore our common humanity. This is the arena in which we can now build the foundations of "a truly free and ecological society."

Unlike classical anarchists, Bookchin proposes a structured and hyper-democratic political system, built on majority voting. It begins with popular assemblies, convened independently of the state, open to anyone from the neighborhood who wants to join. As more assemblies form, they create confederations whose powers are not devolved downward but delegated upward. The assemblies send delegates to represent them at confederal councils, but these delegates have no powers of their own: they may only convey, coordinate, and administer the decisions handed up to them. Unlike conventional elected officials, these delegates can be recalled at any time. In Bookchin's vision, these confederations would grow increasingly autonomous—offering an alternative model of stewardship that prioritizes local self-governance, ecological sustainability, and social justice over the objectives of the state.

Bookchin sees these assemblies as gradually acquiring control over elements of the local economy. Civic banks would fund land purchases and enterprises owned by the community. Funds would be reinvested within communities rather than being pumped into offshore holdings, reinforcing and extending the "commons" (a concept we'll circle back to shortly). The aim is to replace not only statecraft but also economic dominion.

His approach became a major inspiration in the autonomous region in northeastern Syria widely known as Rojava.[2] After local people defeated the ISIL terrorists and the Syrian government withdrew its troops to fight its civil war elsewhere, from 2012 the Rojavans took the chance to build their own politics. Under extraordinarily difficult circumstances, they created a politics in which people have more freedom and control than anywhere in the surrounding regions. It is by no means a perfect republic, but through deliberative democracy—drawing citizens together to discuss and solve their predicaments in person—its people have succeeded in putting Bookchin's ideas to work on a level that many had dismissed as impossible.

This is one of the extraordinary features of deliberative, participatory democracy: it tends to work better in practice than it does in theory. Many of the obstacles that critics imagine dissolve, as people are transformed by the process in which they engage.

A classic example is the practice of "participatory budgeting" in Porto Alegre, southern Brazil. During its peak years (1989–2004), before the system was curtailed by a more hostile local government, it transformed the life of the city.[3] Over these years, citizens were able to decide how the city's entire investment budget should be spent. The process was designed by the city's government and its people working together. It was allowed to evolve as citizens suggested improvements. The budget discussions were open to everyone, and a remarkable 50,000 people a year participated.

Corruption was almost eliminated whereas human welfare and public services were greatly improved.[4] Allowing the people to decide how the money was spent ensured that it went to where it was needed the most—greatly improving sanitation, clean water, green space, health, and education, and transforming the lives of the poor. Porto Alegre, having failed badly in the past, became the Brazilian state capital with the highest ranking on the human development index.

The more people engaged, the wider and deeper their political understanding became. Short-termism was replaced by long-term thinking: an essential pivot if we are to confront chronic public-health issues such as obesity or diseases of despair, address the precipitous decline of our public education systems, or tackle environmental breakdown. The decisions made by the people's assemblies were greener, fairer, wiser, and more distributive than those the city government had previously made.

Programs like Porto Alegre's have stimulated experimentation around "citizens' assemblies" and other forms of deliberative democracy. Similar political projects (although not as far reaching) have been adopted in Taiwan ("vTaiwan"),[5] Madrid ("Decide Madrid"),[6] Barcelona ("Decidim Barcelona"),[7] Lisbon ("Lisboa Participa"),[8] Brussels ("the G1000 Citizen's Summit"),[9] Melbourne ("Future Melbourne"),[10] Finland ("Open Ministry"),[11] and Seoul (participatory budgeting)[12]—all of which allow for some form of participatory governance, budgeting, policy creation, or urban planning.

Why does participatory decision-making work better than we might imagine? Perhaps because the current system of domination persuades us of our own ineptitude and incapacity. The culture wars whipped up by governments and media, then fought between people with similar socioeconomic interests, are made possible by our exclusion from meaningful power. We have few opportunities to engage creatively with one another in building better communities. Disempowerment sets us apart, while shared, equal decision-making brings us together.

Murray Bookchin's prescriptions are no panacea. He fails to deal adequately with transnational issues, especially the problems of global capital, global supply chains, defense against aggressive states, and the need for universal action on global crises (such as climate and ecological breakdown). Although he rejects this approach, we feel that the participatory democracy he advocates can coexist with elements of representative democracy, allowing us to address issues that extend beyond our borders. But representative democracy also requires radical innovation.

The first, most urgent and important step is campaign-finance reform—we must stop the rich from buying political outcomes. One obvious solution is to create a political funding system in which parties charge members the same small, fixed annual fee (people below a certain income threshold could, if they chose, pay less) and are allowed no other forms of funding. This would provide political parties with an incentive to expand their memberships, and citizens with a major incentive to join, as their small fees would not be drowned out by far greater sums provided by plutocrats.

While this proposed solution may seem simple, a fair and democratic system would also need to address the various workarounds that plutocrats already use to avoid political spending limits, such as Super PACs (Political Action Committees) that enable unlimited spending on campaigns, as long as there is no "direct coordination" between the "independent" group raising and spending the money and political candidates or parties;[13] [14] the use of dark-money campaigns; and other loopholes. It needs to be accompanied by radical standards of disclosure and transparency.

Of course, none of this will happen automatically or without encountering great resistance. Alongside the traditional tools of protest and mobilization, we urgently need to develop a wider range of social experiments like those of Porto Alegre and Rojava—making use of sympathetic local, municipal, and national governments wherever they arise. As the benefits of a much richer, more participatory democracy become apparent, more and more people will wonder why they can't have it as well.

A politics such as this recognizes that society, like a rainforest or a financial network, is a complex adaptive system. The standard political model treats society as if it were a simple system, with governments seeking to control the fantastic complexity of human life from the center, by pulling magic levers and dispatching instructions from on high. But the political and economic systems they create are, simultaneously, highly unstable and lacking in dynamism. Like a mismanaged ecosystem, the current political system is both susceptible to collapse and unable to regenerate itself.

Participatory, deliberative democracy is better matched to the dynamics of a complex, self-regulating system. By dispersing and distributing decision-making, it is likely to enhance resilience, preventing the development of what systems theorists call "dominant nodes": institutions or people with excessive power or influence.

Deliberative democracy is not a luxury. We see it as an essential means of defending ourselves from both oligarchy and systemic collapse. Participation in politics is not a gift for which we should beg. It is our right.

24.

PRIVATE SUFFICIENCY, PUBLIC LUXURY

One of the fairy-tale promises of capitalism is that everyone can aspire to private luxury. Neoliberalism then doubles down on this story, claiming that the more private luxury the rich accumulate, the better it will be for everybody. But as we have seen, there simply isn't enough physical space or ecological capacity for everyone to live as the wealthy do. Some own mansions and private estates, ranches and islands—but only because others can't. If we all owned private jets and yachts, the planet would swiftly become uninhabitable. By asserting the right to private luxury, the very rich deprive other people of basic necessities.

So does this mean that no one should aspire to luxury? On the contrary, it means that *everyone* should. Not private luxury, but *public* luxury. While there is not enough space or resources on Earth for everyone to enjoy private luxury, there is enough to provide everyone with magnificent public parks, gardens, hospitals, swimming pools, beaches, art galleries, libraries, tennis courts, transport systems, playgrounds, and community centers. We should each have our own small domains—we should enjoy private sufficiency—but when we want to spread our wings, we can, through public luxury, do so without seizing resources from other people. At the heart of our new restoration story, our politics of belonging, is the notion of *private sufficiency, public luxury*.[1]

We can build public luxury through a combination of the commons and national spending. In other words, on two levels: the community and the state.

The commons is neither market nor state, capitalism nor Communism. It is defined by David Bollier and Silke Helfrich in their book *Free, Fair and Alive* as "a social form that enables people to enjoy freedom without repressing others, enact fairness without bureaucratic control . . . and assert sovereignty without nationalism."[2] The commons are controlled by communities, which devise and implement the rules that govern them. They are an insurgency of social power, in which we come together as equals to confront our shared predicaments.

In many societies, the commons were once the dominant economic mode, before they were captured by capitalist predation, concentrated in the hands of a few, then sliced and bundled for sale to others. Today they persist in many forms, such as community forests or fishing grounds, community parks and play areas, community broadband and energy cooperatives, open-source software, or the shared land for growing fruit and vegetables that in Britain is called "allotments." A commons can't be sold or given away. Its benefits are shared equally among the members of the community. It is the community as a whole that inherits it, generation by generation, and every generation has a duty to keep it in good order.

We will still need the state to provide healthcare, education, and an economic safety net, to distribute wealth between communities, to prevent private interest from becoming too powerful, to defend us from threats (it currently performs these functions poorly, by design). But when we rely on the state alone, we find ourselves sorted into silos of provisioning, and highly vulnerable to "cuts"— restrictions on our access to the resources we might otherwise share more equitably. Rich social lives are replaced with cold, transactional relations.

Community is not a substitute for the state, but an essential complement. Through the commons, operating alongside the state, we can find meaning, purpose, and satisfaction by working together to enhance the lives of all.

For all of this to happen, the excessive accumulation of private wealth will need to be discouraged. The Belgian philosopher Ingrid Robeyns has a term for this: *limitarianism*.[3] Just as there is a poverty line below which no one should fall, she argues that there is a wealth line above which no one should rise—as neither society nor Earth systems can any longer withstand the assaults of plutocracy. The obvious means of breaking the patrimonial spiral of accumulation, of preventing a small number of people from helping themselves to a disproportionate share of space and resources, and of defending politics from the excessive power of the rich, is wealth taxes. It's a simple and effective proposal (as demonstrated during the Second World War). Perhaps it's not surprising, however, that few people in public life are prepared to discuss it.

In order to set this virtuous circle turning, the political and economic domination of the super-wealthy will need to be disrupted. No one is suggesting that this will be easy— far from it—but the process can become self-reinforcing. Enhanced democracy reduces economic inequality; enhanced equality bolsters democracy.

For all the claims of neoliberalism, there is no natural law that dictates the rich should run the world. Their dominance is sustained only by our collective fear, and our failure of political imagination.

25.

THE TIPPING POINT

So how do we get from here to there? How do we, in the predicament in which we find ourselves, build the new political and economic systems that will enhance our lives while protecting the living planet? How do we do this, moreover, before Earth systems collapse?

The task looks impossible as long as we continue to treat society's complex system as if it were a simple one. This is the grand mistake that progressive politicians and campaigners have made. Across almost the entire spectrum of polite resistance, the theory of change is wrong.

Although seldom openly articulated, the theory goes something like this:

There is too little time, and the ask is too big, to try to change the system. People aren't ready for it, and we have to meet them where they are. We can't afford to scare away our members, to lose votes or contributions, or provoke a fight with powerful interests. So the only realistic approach is incrementalism. We will campaign issue by issue, sector by sector, seeking gradual improvements. Eventually, the small asks will add up to the broader change we seek, and deliver the world we want.

For example, environmentalists tell us we face an unprecedented, existential crisis, while simultaneously asking us to recycle our bottle tops and switch to paper drinking straws. Progressive politicians have issued dire warnings about the collapse of living standards and the rise of the far right, while offering only to tweak the neoliberal system that delivers these outcomes. By failing to match their solutions to the scale of the problems, they treat us like idiots—and we know it. Across most of the progressive spectrum, a timid reluctance to articulate what we really want—and a mistaken belief that people aren't ready to hear anything more challenging—condemns us to failure.

But while campaigners and progressive politicians have been playing solitaire, power has been playing poker. The radical right's insurgency has swept all before it, crushing the administrative state; destroying public protections; capturing the courts, the electoral system, the infrastructure of government; and restricting the right to protest. While we persuaded ourselves that there was no time for system change, they proved us wrong by changing *everything*.

The problem was never that system change is too big an ask or that it takes too long. The problem is that incrementalism is too *small* an ask. Not just too small to drive transformation; not just too small to stop the tsunami of revolutionary change rolling in from the opposite direction; but also too small to break the conspiracy of silence surrounding our great predicament. Only a demand for system change, directly confronting the powers driving us to societal despair and planetary destruction, has the potential to confront the scale of our problems. Only a big ask—a very big one—will inspire and mobilize the millions of people required to transform our political and economic system.

There was never time for incrementalism. Far from being a shortcut to the change we want to see, it is the morass into which ambition sinks. System change, as the neoliberals and the new demagogues have proven, is, and has always been, the only fast and effective means of transformation.

Just as a financial system or an ecosystem can flip suddenly from one state of equilibrium to another, so can societies. Like these systems, societies have self-reinforcing properties that stabilize them and damp down shocks within a particular range of stress, but destabilize them, amplifying shocks, when stress rises beyond a certain point. Like natural systems, if they are driven past their tipping points, they can flip with astonishing speed. The difference is that social tipping can be beneficial.

It has happened many times before: sudden, sweeping changes have taken place, though they seemed unimaginable shortly before they happened. Think of smoking. Not long ago, smoking in public places was acceptable almost everywhere. When people spoke of decisions being made in "smoke-filled rooms," they were not exaggerating. Public buildings, offices, trains, buses, airplanes, theaters, pubs, bars, school bathrooms, and teachers' lounges—even restaurants—were filled with a suffocating fug. It seemed to just be "the way things were": a high proportion of the population smoked, and politicians didn't have the guts to do anything about it, for fear of the votes and taxes they might lose.[1] Today, the few remaining smokers linger in alleyways near the dumpster, furtively taking a hasty drag as if they were still in high school. The situation has changed entirely, in a remarkably short space of time.

We can see similar effects in other aspects of social change, such as sexual liberation and marriage equality. How did these shifts happen? Advocates and campaigners gradually expanded the concentric circles of people who were committed to new beliefs and practices, until they reached a critical threshold, at which point change cascaded suddenly and unstoppably.

We now have a good idea of where such thresholds might lie. Both observational and experimental data suggest that once roughly 25 percent of the population is committed to change, most of the rest of society quickly joins them.[2] In one experiment, between 72 percent and 100 percent of people swung around, once the critical threshold had been reached, reversing the group's social norms.[3] As the paper reporting this research notes, a large body of work suggests that "the power of small groups comes not from their authority or wealth, but from their commitment to the cause."

This social tipping happens partly as a result of the inherent dynamics of a complex system and partly because we are such social mammals. A critical threshold is reached when a certain proportion of the population changes its views. When others sense that the wind has changed, they tack around to catch it. The majority doesn't need to be persuaded to change—they just don't want to be left behind. We might not even be conscious of making the shift: it simply becomes the new common sense. Even those who were once opposed to bans on smoking in public places, or the idea that gay people should have the same rights to marry as straight people, fall into line with the new social consensus. Some will go on to claim, and to believe, that they always supported such shifts. Time and again, on issues ranging from racial equality, to LGBTQ+ rights, to traditional gender roles and family structures, to mental-health awareness, to sexual harassment and assault, to marijuana legalization—we've seen these shifts in collective perception. After the War, everyone became a member of the Resistance.

Of course, this raises the issue of what we mean by "a society." In some places, "the nation" functions as a reasonable description of "society." But others—the United States in particular—have become so divided that they now appear to operate and identify as two separate and distinct societies. We cannot expect that a social tipping that transforms one-half of this divided nation will automatically transform the other. But we need to act where and how we can to create, wherever possible, poles of resistance and examples of change that can inspire and mobilize our better values: altruism, empathy, community, family, and the pursuit of a more just and equitable world, values to which most people subscribe, regardless of political or religious affiliation. The most important question that humanity has ever faced is whether we can reach the social tipping points before we reach the environmental tipping points.

If we are to reach these social tipping points, our first task is to tear down the cloak of invisibility that shields both neoliberalism and the true nature of capitalism from public view. It is to expose their breaches, their obscurities, and their deceptions. It is to reveal what has been hidden. It is to speak their names.

ACKNOWLEDGMENTS

Many thanks to the people who made this book and the thinking and research behind it possible: Antony Harwood, Anthony Arnove, Chloe Currens, Amanda Cook, Ruth Pietroni, Katie Berry, Richard Mason, Fiona Rowe, Lucas Sabean, Moritz Riede, Jo Haward, Jeremy Lent, Chris Tanigawa, Liza Stepanovich, Liana Parry Faughnan, Aubrey Khan, Chris Brand, Penny Simon, Kim Lew, Julie Cepler, the *Guardian*'s comment editors, our families—Rebecca, Hanna, and Martha, and Pamela and Levon—and many supportive friends and thinkers.

NOTES

CHAPTER 2
THE "FREE" MARKET

1. Adam Smith, 1759. *The Theory of Moral Sentiments*. London and Edinburgh.
2. Facundo Alvaredo, Lucas Chancel, Thomas Piketty, Emmanuel Saez, and Gabriel Zucman, 2020. *Toward a System of Distributional National Accounts: Methods and Global Inequality Estimates from WID.world*. Economie et Statistique / Economics and Statistics, Institut National de la Statistique et des Etudes Economiques (INSEE), issue 517-518-5, pp. 41–59. https://eml.berkeley.edu/~saez/Alvaredo-et-al_04-ES_517-518-519-ENWeb.pdf.
3. Paul Verhaeghe (trans. Jane Hedley-Prole), 2014. *What About Me? The Struggle for Identity in a Market-Based Society*. Scribe, London.

CHAPTER 3
THE FAIRY TALE OF CAPITALISM

1. Jason W. Moore, 2010. "Madeira, sugar, and the conquest of nature in the 'first' sixteenth century. Part II: From regional crisis to commodity frontier, 1506–1530," *Review* (Fernand Braudel Center), vol. 33, no. 1, pp. 1–24. https://www.jstor.org/stable/41427556.
2. Ibid.
3. Karl Polanyi, 1944. *The Great Transformation*. Farrar & Rinehart, New York.
4. Moore, "Madeira, sugar, and the conquest of nature in the 'first' sixteenth century."
5. Ajai Sreevatsan, November 19, 2018. "British Raj siphoned out $45 trillion from India: Utsa Patnaik." *Mint*. https://www.livemint

.com/Companies/HNZA71LNVNNVXQ1eaIKu6M/British -Raj-siphoned-out-45-trillion-from-India-Utsa-Patna.html.

6. Laleh Khalili, September 23, 2021. "How to get rich," *London Review of Books*. https://www.lrb.co.uk/the-paper/v43/n18/laleh -khalili/how-to-get-rich.

7. Michael Thomson, Alexandros Kentikelenis, and Thomas Stubbs, 2017. "Structural adjustment programs adversely affect vulnerable populations: a systematic-narrative review of their effect on child and maternal health." *Public Health Review*, vol. 38, no. 13. https://publichealthreviews.biomedcentral.com/articles/10.1186 /s40985-017-0059-2.

8. Tax Justice Network. "What is transfer pricing?" https://taxjustice .net/faq/what-is-transfer-pricing.

9. Dev Kar and Joseph Spanjers, December 2015. "Illicit financial flows from developing countries: 2004–2013." *Global Financial Integrity*. https://gfintegrity.org/report/illicit-financial-flows-from -developing-countries-2004-2013.

10. Victor Tangermann, February 25, 2019. "Jeff Bezos: in the future, we'll live in 'giant space colonies.'" *The Byte*. futurism.com. https:// futurism.com/the-byte/jeff-bezos-future-giant-space-colonies.

11. Moore, "Madeira, sugar, and the conquest of nature in the 'first' sixteenth century."

12. John Locke, 1689. *Second Treatise of Government*. Awnsham Churchill, London. https://www.gutenberg.org/files/7370/7370 -h/7370-h.htm.

13. Donald L. Fixico, 2018 (updated July 11, 2023). "When Native Americans were slaughtered in the name of 'civilization.'" History .com. https://www.history.com/news/native-americans-genocide -united-states.

CHAPTER 4
RISE OF THE NEOLIBERAL INTERNATIONAL

1. Walter Lippmann Colloquium, 1938. wikilibéral.org. https:// en.wikipedia.org/wiki/Colloque_Walter_Lippmann.

2. Friedrich A. Hayek, 1944. *The Road to Serfdom*. Routledge Press, London.

3. Ludwig von Mises, 1944. *Bureaucracy*. William Hodge & Co., Edinburgh.

4. Friedrich A. Hayek, April 1945. *The Road to Serfdom*, a *Reader's Digest* condensed version, reprinted by the Institute of Economic Affairs, 2001. https://www.iea.org.uk/sites/default/files /publications/files/upldbook43pdf.pdf.

5. *The Road to Serfdom in Cartoons.* Thought Starter series, no. 118, 1945. Published originally in *Look* magazine (General Motors). https://archive.org/details/RoadToSerfdomInCartoonsLook MagazineFrederickHayek10.

6. Kim Phillips-Fein, October 12, 2014. "Friedrich von Hayek, Thomas Piketty, and the search for political economy." Political Research Associates. https://politicalresearch.org/2014/10/12 /friedrich-von-hayek-thomas-piketty-and-search-political -economy.

7. Brendan Montague, September 17, 2014. "Starting with a mistake, a remorseless logician can end up in Bedlham." *DeSmog.* https:// www.desmog.com/2014/09/17/starting-mistake-remorseless -logician-can-end-bedlham.

8. The Mont Pelerin Society (MPS). *DeSmog.* https://www.desmog .com/mont-pelerin-society.

9. Daniel Stedman Jones, 2012. *Masters of the Universe: Hayek, Friedman, and the Birth of Neoliberal Politics.* Princeton University Press, Princeton, NJ.

10. Ibid.

11. Ibid.

12. George Monbiot, April 15, 2016. "Neoliberalism—the ideology at the root of all our problems." *The Guardian.* https://www .theguardian.com/books/2016/apr/15/neoliberalism-ideology -problem-george-monbiot.

13. Stedman Jones, *Masters of the Universe.*

14. Monbiot, "Neoliberalism."

15. Stedman Jones, *Masters of the Universe.*

16. Ibid.

17. *The Road to Serfdom in Cartoons.*

18. Vivian Gornick, November 16, 2017. "Little house, small government—how Laura Ingalls Wilder's frontier vision of freedom and survival lives on in Trump's America." *The New Republic.* https://newrepublic.com/article/145410/little-house-small -government-laura-ingalls-wilder-frontier-vision-freedom -survival-lives-trump-america.

19. Julie Tharp and Jeff Kleiman, 2000. "*Little House on the Prairie and the myth of self-reliance.*" *Transformations: The Journal of Inclusive Scholarship and Pedagogy*, vol. 11, no. 1, pp. 55–64. https://www.jstor.org/stable/43587224.

20. Christine Woodside, September 11, 2016. "How *Little House on the Prairie* built modern conservatism." *Politico Magazine*. https://www.politico.com/magazine/story/2016/09/little-house-on-the-prairie-conservatism-214237.

21. Friedrich Hayek, 1960. *The Constitution of Liberty*. University of Chicago Press, Chicago.

22. Noam Chomsky, 2017. *Requiem for the American Dream: The 10 Principles of Concentration of Wealth & Power*. Seven Stories Press, New York.

23. Jeffrey Rosen, October 2018. "America is living James Madison's nightmare." *The Atlantic*. https://www.theatlantic.com/magazine/archive/2018/10/james-madison-mob-rule/568351.

24. Milton Friedman, February 17, 1951. "Neo-liberalism and its prospects." *Farmand*, pp. 89–93. https://miltonfriedman.hoover.org/internal/media/dispatcher/214957/full.

25. James R. Crotty, 1983. "On Keynes and capital flight." *Journal of Economic Literature*, vol. 21, no. 1, pp. 59–65. https://www.jstor.org/stable/2724749.

26. Christoffer J. P. Zoeller, 2019. "Closing the gold window: the end of Bretton Woods as a contingency plan." *Politics & Society*, vol. 47, no. 1, pp. 3–22. https://journals.sagepub.com/doi/10.1177/0032329218823648.

27. Jeff Nussbaum, October 16, 2015. "The night New York saved itself from bankruptcy." *The New Yorker*. https://www.newyorker.com/news/news-desk/the-night-new-york-saved-itself-from-bankruptcy.

28. Kim Phillips-Fein, May 6, 2013. "The legacy of the 1970s fiscal crisis." *The Nation*. https://www.thenation.com/article/archive/legacy-1970s-fiscal-crisis.

29. Stedman Jones, *Masters of the Universe*.

30. "Sterling devalued and the IMF loan." The Cabinet Papers, The National Archives (UK). https://www.nationalarchives.gov.uk/cabinetpapers/themes/sterling-devalued-imf-loan.htm.

31. Steve H. Hanke, March 5, 2001. "Reagan the intellectual." *Forbes*. https://www.forbes.com/forbes/2001/0305/080.html.

32. Steve H. Hanke, August 6, 2007. "Reflections on Reagan the intellectual." Cato Institute/Globe Asia. https://www.cato.org /commentary/reflections-reagan-intellectual.

33. Stephen Metcalf, August 18, 2017. "Neoliberalism: the idea that swallowed the world." *The Guardian*. https://www.theguardian .com/news/2017/aug/18/neoliberalism-the-idea-that-changed -the-world.

34. Arthur C. Brooks, April 8, 2013. "Margaret Thatcher was a powerful voice for free enterprise and liberty." American Enterprise Institute. https://www.aei.org/foreign-and-defense-policy/europe -and-eurasia/margaret-thatcher-was-a-powerful-voice-for-free -enterprise-and-liberty.

35. Leonard E. Read, March 3, 2015. "I, pencil." Foundation for Economic Education (FEE). https://fee.org/resources/i-pencil.

CHAPTER 5
THE NEOLIBERAL ERA

1. Nelson Lichtenstein, January 29, 2018. "A fabulous failure: Clinton's 1990s and the origins of our times." *The American Prospect*. https://prospect.org/health/fabulous-failure-clinton-s-1990s -origins-times.

2. Nelson Lichtenstein, September 13, 2023. "Bill Clinton's failure." Princeton University Press, Princeton, NJ. https://press.princeton .edu/ideas/bill-clintons-failure.

3. President William Jefferson Clinton, State of the Union Address, U.S. Capitol, January 23, 2023. The White House. https://clintonwhitehouse4.archives.gov/WH/New/other/sotu .html.

4. Associated Press, October 19, 2012. "Who are top 5 donors to Obama, Romney campaigns?" https://www.politico.com/story /2012/10/who-are-top-5-donors-to-obama-romney-campaigns -082637.

5. *The New York Times*, updated September 13, 2012. "Obama's top fund-raisers." NYT Archive. https://archive.nytimes.com/www .nytimes.com/interactive/2012/09/13/us/politics/obamas-top -fund-raisers.html.

6. Adi Robertson, September 16, 2012. "In Obama campaign, tech industry donors could be outspending their Hollywood counter-

parts." *The Verge*. https://www.theverge.com/2012/9/16/3341412 /obama-tech-industry-fundraisers.

7. Elinor Mills, August 29, 2012. "Microsoft, Google folks are top sources for Obama funds." *CNET*. https://www.cnet.com/tech /tech-industry/microsoft-google-folks-are-top-sources-for -obama-funds.

8. Associated Press, March 26, 2012. "Top Obama donors get to the White House." CNBC. https://www.cnbc.com/id/46858797.

9. Matt Taibbi, February 16, 2011. "Why isn't Wall Street in jail?" *Rolling Stone*. https://www.rollingstone.com/politics/politics-news /why-isnt-wall-street-in-jail-179414.

CHAPTER 6

WHAT'S LIBERAL ABOUT NEOLIBERALISM?

1. Greg Grandin, November 17, 2006. "The road from serfdom." *CounterPunch*. https://www.counterpunch.org/2006/11/17/the -road-from-serfdom.

2. Lauren Aratani, February 15, 2023. "What do we know about the Ohio train derailment and toxic chemical leak?" *The Guardian*. https://www.theguardian.com/world/2023/feb/15/ohio-train -derailment-palestine-toxic-chemical-leak.

3. Jared Rutecki, March 8, 2023. "Illinois is no stranger to train de-railments involving hazardous materials. Could an East Palestine disaster happen here?" WTTW. https://news.wttw.com/2023/03 /08/illinois-no-stranger-train-derailments-involving-hazardous -materials-could-east-palestine.

4. Li Zhou, March 30, 2023. "Why train derailments involving hazardous chemicals keep happening." *Vox*. https://www.vox.com /policy/2023/3/30/23663182/minnesota-train-derailment-east -palestine-hazardous-chemicals.

5. Richard Henry Tawney, 1931. *Equality*. Allen & Unwin, London.

6. Stephen Metcalf, August 18, 2017. "Neoliberalism: the idea that swallowed the world." *The Guardian*. https://www.theguardian .com/news/2017/aug/18/neoliberalism-the-idea-that-changed -the-world.

7. Naomi Klein, 2007. *The Shock Doctrine: The Rise of Disaster Capitalism*. Knopf, Canada, and Penguin, London, 2008.

8. Milton Friedman, December 5, 2005. "The promise of vouchers." *Wall Street Journal.* https://www.wsj.com/articles /SB113374845791113764.

9. Sarah Babb and Alexandros Kentikelenis, 2018. "International financial institutions as agents of neoliberalism," in *The SAGE Handbook of Neoliberalism*, pp. 16–27. SAGE Publications. http://www.kentikelenis.net/uploads/3/1/8/9/31894609 /babbkentikelenis2018-international_financial_institutions_as _agents_of_neoliberalism.pdf.

10. AFL-CIO, September 12, 2014. "How investor-to-state dispute settlement threatens public welfare and undermines democracy." Public Services International. https://www.world-psi.org/en/how -investor-state-dispute-settlement-threatens-public-welfare -and-undermines-democracy.

11. The United Nations Conference on Trade and Development, September 2021. "Investor–state dispute settlement cases: facts and figures 2020." *IIA (International Investment Agreements) Issues Note*, issue 4. https://unctad.org/system/files/official-document /diaepcbinf2021d7_en.pdf.

12. Global Justice Now. ISDS case studies. https://www.globaljustice .org.uk/our-campaigns/trade/corporate-courts/isds-case-studies.

13. Jean Blaylock, June 24, 2022. "What is the energy charter treaty and why do we need to exit?" Global Justice Now. https://www .globaljustice.org.uk/blog/2022/06/energy-charter-treaty.

14. Nia Williams, February 9, 2022. "UPDATE 1—Canada's Alberta province files trade challenge over scrapped Keystone XL pipeline." Reuters. https://www.reuters.com/article/canada -alberta-kxl-idAFL1N2UK221.

15. Scott Sinclair, March 4, 2021. "Trade agreements like NAFTA are a menace to democracy." *Jacobin.* https://jacobin.com/2021/03 /trade-agreements-nafta-isds-canada.

16. The United Nations Conference on Trade and Development. "Investor–state dispute settlement cases."

CHAPTER 7
"RENT" AND OTHER AMBIGUITIES

1. Mike Konczal, Katy Milani, and Ariel Evans, January 2020. "The empirical failures of neoliberalism." The Roosevelt Institute.

https://rooseveltinstitute.org/wp-content/uploads/2020/07/RI
_The-Empirical-Failures-of-Neoliberalism_brief-202001.pdf.

2. Tim Koechlin, 2013. "The rich get richer: Neoliberalism and soaring inequality in the United States." *Challenge*, vol. 56, no. 2, pp. 5–30. https://www.jstor.org/stable/23524375.

3. Matt Bruenig, June 14, 2019. "Top 1% up $21 trillion. Bottom 50% down $900 billion." People's Policy Project. https://www .peoplespolicyproject.org/2019/06/14/top-1-up-21-trillion -bottom-50-down-900-billion.

4. Eric Levitz, June 16, 2019. "The one percent have gotten $21 trillion richer since 1989. The bottom 50% have gotten poorer." *New York Magazine.* https://nymag.com/intelligencer/2019/06/the -fed-just-released-a-damning-indictment-of-capitalism.html.

5. Office for National Statistics, December 5, 2017. "Households sector continues to have the greatest effect on UK net worth. The UK national balance sheet estimates: 2017, Section 6." https:// www.ons.gov.uk/economy/nationalaccounts/uksectoraccounts /bulletins/nationalbalancesheet/2017estimates#households -sector-continues-to-have-the-greatest-effect-on-uk-net-worth.

6. Branko Milanovic, 2011. *The Haves and the Have-Nots: A Brief and Idiosyncratic History of Global Inequality.* Basic Books, New York.

7. Greg Rosalsky, March 22, 2022. "How 'shock therapy' created Russian oligarchs and paved the path for Putin." NPR (National Public Radio). https://www.npr.org/sections/money/2022/03/22 /1087654279/how-shock-therapy-created-russian-oligarchs -and-paved-the-path-for-putin.

8. Ibid.

9. Ibid.

10. Sandra Laville and Helena Horton, December 6, 2022. "Ofwat attacks water firms' lack of investment to cut sewage discharges." *The Guardian.* https://www.theguardian.com/environment/2022 /dec/06/ofwat-attacks-water-firms-lack-of-investment-to-cut -sewage-discharges.

11. Natalie Wexler, January 13, 2019. "Math and science can't take priority over history and civics." *Forbes.* https://www.forbes.com /sites/nataliewexler/2019/01/13/math-and-science-cant-take -priority-over-history-and-civics/?sh=5b84b4b6199e.

12. John Kenneth Galbraith, 1958. *The Affluent Society.* Houghton Mifflin, Boston.

13. Tony Judt, 2010. *Ill Fares the Land*. Penguin, London.

14. Andrew Sayer, 2014. *Why We Can't Afford the Rich*. Policy Press, Bristol, UK.

15. Ian Irvine, May 5, 2019. "The way we were: snobbery." *Prospect Magazine*. https://www.prospectmagazine.co.uk/society/42603/the-way-we-were-snobbery.

16. Judt, *Ill Fares the Land*.

CHAPTER 8
THE REDISTRIBUTION OF WEALTH

1. Simon Szreter, November 2021. "The history of inequality: the deep-acting ideological and institutional influences." Institute for Fiscal Studies Deaton Review of Inequalities. https://ifs.org.uk/inequality/wp-content/uploads/2021/11/IFS-Deaton-Review-The-history-of-inequality-1.pdf.

2. Greg Grandin, November 17, 2006. "The road from serfdom." *CounterPunch*. https://www.counterpunch.org/2006/11/17/the-road-from-serfdom.

3. Dante Contreras and Ricardo Ffrench-Davis, 2012. "Policy regimes, inequality, poverty and growth: the Chilean experience, 1973–2010." United Nations University World Institute for Development Economics Research (UNU-WIDER), Working Paper no. 2012/04. https://www.econstor.eu/handle/10419/81078.

4. Carter C. Price and Kathryn A. Edwards, 2020. "Trends in income from 1975 to 2018." RAND Corporation, no. WR-A516-1. https://www.rand.org/pubs/working_papers/WRA516-1.html.

5. Laurie Macfarlane, November 3, 2020. "Six charts that reveal America's deep divides." *openDemocracy*. https://www.opendemocracy.net/en/oureconomy/six-charts-that-reveal-americas-deep-divides.

6. Resolution Foundation, March 20, 2023. "15 years of economic stagnation has left workers across Britain with an £11,000 a year lost wages gap." https://www.resolutionfoundation.org/press-releases/15-years-of-economic-stagnation-has-left-workers-across-britain-with-an-11000-a-year-lost-wages-gap.

7. Oxfam International, January 17, 2022. "Ten richest men double their fortunes in pandemic while incomes of 99 percent

of humanity fall." https://www.oxfam.org/en/press-releases/ten
-richest-men-double-their-fortunes-pandemic-while-incomes
-99-percent-humanity.

8.   Carolina Sánchez-Páramo et al., October 7, 2021. "COVID-19
leaves a legacy of rising poverty and widening inequality." *World
Bank Blogs.* https://blogs.worldbank.org/developmenttalk/covid
-19-leaves-legacy-rising-poverty-and-widening-inequality.

9.   Chiara Putaturo, January 18, 2023. "The super-rich pay lower
taxes than you—and here's how they do it . . ." *Views & Voices*
(Oxfam). https://views-voices.oxfam.org.uk/2023/01/how-super
-rich-pay-lower-taxes-than-you.

10. Report prepared for the G20 Employment Working Group, An-
talya, Turkey, February 26–27, 2015. "The labor share in G20
economies." International Labor Organisation for Economic
Co-operation and Development with contributions from the International Monetary Fund and World Bank Group. https://
www.oecd.org/g20/topics/employment-and-social-policy/The
-Labor-Share-in-G20-Economies.pdf.

11. Emmanuel Saez and Gabriel Zucman, 2020. "The rise of
income and wealth inequality in America: evidence from
distributional macroeconomic accounts." *Journal of Economic Perspectives*, vol. 34, no. 4, pp. 3–26. https://eml.berkeley.edu/~saez
/SaezZucman2020JEP.pdf.

12. GDP growth (annual %). World Bank national accounts data,
and OECD National Accounts data files, 2023. https://data
.worldbank.org/indicator/NY.GDP.MKTP.KD.ZG.

13. John Maynard Keynes, 1932. *Economic Possibilities for Our Grand-
children* (1930). Essays in Persuasion. Harcourt Brace, New York,
pp. 358–73. https://www.aspeninstitute.org/wp-content/uploads
/files/content/upload/Intro_and_Section_I.pdf.

14. Jason Hickel, March 19, 2020. "Outgrowing growth: why quality
of life, not GDP, should be our measure of success." *The Corre-
spondent.* https://thecorrespondent.com/357/outgrowing-growth
-why-quality-of-life-not-gdp-should-be-our-measure-of
-success.

15. Richard A. Easterlin and Kelsey J. O'Connor, September 6, 2022.
"Explaining happiness trends in Europe." *PNAS (Proceedings of
the National Academy of Sciences)*, vol. 119, no. 37. https://pubmed
.ncbi.nlm.nih.gov/36067317.

16. David Kotz, 2008. "Contradictions of economic growth in the neoliberal era: accumulation and crisis in the contemporary U.S. economy." *Review of Radical Political Economics*, vol. 40, issue 2, pp. 174–88. https://people.umass.edu/dmkotz/Contradictions _07_05.pdf.

CHAPTER 9
THE CRISIS OF DEMOCRACY

1. William Davies, April 30, 2017. "Essay: populism and the limits of neoliberalism." *London School of Economics and Political Science.* https://blogs.lse.ac.uk/europpblog/2017/04/30/essay-populism -and-the-limits-of-neoliberalism-by-william-davies.

2. Tony Judt, 2010. *Ill Fares the Land.* Penguin, London.

3. Richard J. Evans, February 28, 2017. "A warning from history: a new biography of Hitler reminds us that there is more than one way to destroy a democracy." *The Nation.* https://www.thenation .com/article/archive/the-ways-to-destroy-democracy.

4. Christopher Hope, September 22, 2020. "Culture secretary: the National Trust should 'preserve' our heritage, not criticise Churchill." *The Telegraph.* https://www.telegraph.co.uk/politics /2020/09/22/culture-secretary-national-trust-should-preserve -heritage-not.

5. Martin Beckford and Connor Stringer, June 22, 2023. "Equalities Minister Kemi Badenoch demands snap inspection over 'pupil identifying as cat' row." *Daily Mail.* https://www.dailymail.co.uk /news/article-12224631/Equalities-Minister-Kemi-Badenoch -demands-snap-inspection-pupil-identifying-cat-row.html.

6. Joshua Keating, March 3, 2021. "Less than 20 percent of the world's population now lives in a 'free' country." *Slate.* https:// slate.com/news-and-politics/2021/03/freedom-house-freedom -in-the-world.html.

7. Grace Blakeley, June 17, 2023. "True democracy is incompatible with capitalism." *Jacobin.* https://jacobin.com/2023/06/democracy -retreat-capitalism-authoritarianism-crisis.

8. Ibid.

9. Freedom House, March 3, 2021. "New report: the global decline in democracy has accelerated." https://freedomhouse.org/article /new-report-global-decline-democracy-has-accelerated.

10. Grace Blakeley, June 15, 2023. "No, capitalism isn't democratic." *Tribune*. https://tribunemag.co.uk/2023/06/no-capitalism-isnt -democratic.

CHAPTER 10
THE LONELINESS OF NEOLIBERALISM

1. Paul Verhaeghe (trans. Jane Hedley-Prole), 2014. *What About Me? The Struggle for Identity in a Market-Based Society*. Scribe, London.

2. Carol Graham, February 10, 2021. "America's crisis of despair: a federal task force for economic recovery and societal well-being." Brookings Institution. https://www.brookings.edu/articles /americas-crisis-of-despair-a-federal-task-force-for-economic -recovery-and-societal-well-being.

3. Mohammed Umer Waris, March 20, 2023. "Deaths of despair: an urgent call for a collective response to the crisis in U.S. life expectancy." *KevinMD*. https://www.kevinmd.com/2023/03 /deaths-of-despair-an-urgent-call-for-a-collective-response-to -the-crisis-in-u-s-life-expectancy.html.

4. Office of Communication, November 17, 2021. "Drug overdose deaths in the U.S. top 100,000 annually." Centers for Disease Control and Prevention (CDC), National Center for Health Statistics. https://www.cdc.gov/nchs/pressroom/nchs_press_releases/2021 /20211117.htm.

5. Graham, "America's crisis of despair."

6. Waris, "Deaths of despair."

7. Covid Mutual Aid, Local Groups. https://covidmutualaid.org /local-groups.

8. Works & Days, Kalantzis & Cope. "Margaret Thatcher: there's no such thing as society." 1987 excerpt from interview for *Woman's Own*. https://newlearningonline.com/new-learning/chapter -4/neoliberalism-more-recent-times/margaret-thatcher-theres -no-such-thing-as-society.

9. Thomas Hobbes, 1651. *Leviathan, or the Matter, Form and Power of a Commonwealth Ecclesiastical and Civil*. London.

10. George Monbiot, November 7, 2011. "The self-attribution fallacy." https://www.monbiot.com/2011/11/07/the-self-attribution -fallacy.

11. Paolo Riva, James H. Wirth, and Kipling D. Williams, 2011.

"The consequences of pain: the social and physical pain overlap on psychological responses." *European Journal of Social Psychology*, vol. 41, issue 6, pp. 681–87. https://onlinelibrary.wiley.com/doi /abs/10.1002/ejsp.837.

12. Naomi I. Eisenberger, 2012. "The pain of social disconnection: examining the shared neural underpinnings of physical and social pain." *Nature Reviews Neuroscience*, vol. 13, pp. 421–34. https:// www.nature.com/articles/nrn3231.

13. John A. Sturgeon and Alex J. Zautra, 2016. "Social pain and physical pain: shared paths to resilience." *Pain Management*, vol. 6, no. 1, pp. 63–74. https://www.ncbi.nlm.nih.gov/pmc/articles /PMC4869967.

14. Pavel Goldstein, Irit Weissman-Fogel, and Simone G. Shamay-Tsoory, 2017. "The role of touch in regulating inter-partner physiological coupling during empathy for pain." *Scientific Reports*, vol. 7, article no. 3252. https://www.nature.com/articles/s41598 -017-03627-7.

15. Johann Hari, 2015. *Chasing the Scream*. Bloomsbury, London.

16. Franklin D. McMillan, 2016. "The psychobiology of social pain: evidence for a neurocognitive overlap with physical pain and welfare implications for social animals with special attention to the domestic dog (Canis familiaris)." *Physiology & Behavior*, vol. 167, pp. 154–71. https://www.sciencedirect.com/science/article/abs /pii/S0031938416305583.

17. Byron Egeland and Alan Sroufe, 1981. "Developmental sequelae of maltreatment in infancy," *New Directions for Child and Adolescent Development*, vol. 1, 981, no. 11, pp. 77–92.

18. Lixia Ge et al., 2017. "Social isolation, loneliness and their relationships with depressive symptoms: a population-based study." *PLOS ONE*, vol. 12, no. 8. https://journals.plos.org/plosone /article?id=10.1371/journal.pone.0182145.

19. Chloé Motillon-Toudic et al., 2022. "Social isolation and suicide risk: literature review and perspectives." *European Psychiatry*, vol. 65, no. 1, E65. https://www.cambridge.org/core/journals /european-psychiatry/article/social-isolation-and-suicide-risk -literature-review-and-perspectives/4069F339C7A480FC8B4E C1667A3F092C.

20. Catherine E. Robb et al., 2020. "Associations of social isolation with anxiety and depression during the early COVID-19 pan-

demic: a survey of older adults in London, UK." *Frontiers in Psychiatry*, vol. 11. https://www.frontiersin.org/articles/10.3389/fpsyt.2020.591120/full.

21. Keiko Murakami et al. 2022. "Social isolation and insomnia among pregnant women in Japan: the Tohoku Medical Megabank Project Birth and three-generation cohort study." *Sleep Health*, vol. 8, no. 6, pp. 714–20. https://www.sciencedirect.com/science/article/abs/pii/S2352721822001474.

22. John T. Cacioppo and Stephanie Cacioppo, 2014. "Social relationships and health: the toxic effects of perceived social isolation." *Social and Personality Psychology Compass*, vol. 8, no. 2, pp. 58–72. https://compass.onlinelibrary.wiley.com/doi/abs/10.1111/spc3.12087.

23. Joel Salinas et al., 2022. "Association of loneliness with 10-year dementia risk and early markers of vulnerability for neurocognitive decline." *Neurology*, vol. 98, 13, e1337–e1348. https://n.neurology.org/content/98/13/e1337.abstract.

24. Jeffrey A. Lam et al., 2021. "Neurobiology of loneliness: a systematic review." *Neuropsychopharmacology*, vol. 46, pp. 1,873–87. https://www.nature.com/articles/s41386-021-01058-7.

25. Sam Hodgson et al., 2020. "Loneliness, social isolation, cardiovascular disease and mortality: a synthesis of the literature and conceptual framework." *Journal of the Royal Society of Medicine*, vol. 113, no. 5, pp. 185–92. https://journals.sagepub.com/doi/full/10.1177/0141076820918236.

26. Stephanie Cacioppo, John P. Capitanio, and John T. Cacioppo, 2014. "Toward a neurology of loneliness." *Psychological Bulletin*, vol. 140, no. 6, pp. 1,464–504. https://psycnet.apa.org/record/2014-37731-001.

27. Feifei Bu et al., 2020. "A longitudinal analysis of loneliness, social isolation and falls amongst older people in England." *Scientific Reports*, vol. 10, article no. 20064. https://www.nature.com/articles/s41598-020-77104-z.

28. Julianne Holt-Lunstad, Timothy B. Smith, and J. Bradley Layton, 2010. "Social relationships and mortality risk: a meta-analytic review." *PLOS Medicine*, vol. 7, no. 7. https://journals.plos.org/plosmedicine/article?id=10.1371/journal.pmed.1000316.

CHAPTER 11
INVISIBLE DOCTRINE—INVISIBLE BACKERS

1. The Nanny State Index, May 10, 2017. "UK is second worst country in the EU for nanny state interference." IEA (Institute of Economic Affairs). https://iea.org.uk/media/uk-is-second-worst-country-in-the-eu-for-nanny-state-interference.

2. Jamie Doward, June 1, 2013. "Health groups dismayed by news 'big tobacco' funded right-wing thinktanks." *The Guardian.* https://www.theguardian.com/society/2013/jun/01/thinktanks-big-tobacco-funds-smoking.

3. Tobacco Tactics, October 17, 2023. Institute of Economic Affairs. https://tobaccotactics.org/article/institute-of-economic-affairs.

4. Jane Mayer, 2016. *Dark Money.* Doubleday, New York.

5. Suzanne Goldenberg, October 13, 2010. "Tea Party movement: billionaire Koch brothers who helped it grow." *The Guardian.* https://www.theguardian.com/world/2010/oct/13/tea-party-billionaire-koch-brothers.

6. Charles Koch and family. "October 2023." *Forbes.* https://www.forbes.com/profile/charles-koch/?sh=ae3a6b457d70.

7. Sean Ross, September 20, 2023. "Top 10 wealthiest families in the world." Investopedia. https://www.investopedia.com/articles/insights/052416/top-10-wealthiest-families-world.asp.

8. "Koch Industries pollution: Koch and the environment." Greenpeace. https://www.greenpeace.org/usa/fighting-climate-chaos/climate-deniers/koch-industries/koch-industries-pollution.

9. Bill McKibben, March 10, 2016. "The Koch brothers' new brand." *The New York Review.* https://www.nybooks.com/articles/2016/03/10/koch-brothers-new-brand.

10. Mayer, *Dark Money.*

11. Jane Mayer, August 23, 2010. "Covert operations." *The New Yorker.* https://www.newyorker.com/magazine/2010/08/30/covert-operations.

12. "The Heritage Foundation: Koch Industries climate denial front group." Greenpeace. https://www.greenpeace.org/usa/fighting-climate-chaos/climate-deniers/front-groups/the-heritage-foundation.

13. Charles Heatherly, 1981. *Mandate for Leadership.* The Heritage Foundation, Washington, DC.

14. Margaret Shapiro, November 22, 1984. "Mandate II." *The Washington Post*. https://www.washingtonpost.com/archive/politics/1984/11/22/mandate-ii/ee2ede6b-86c0-4180-8e94-3d4a533a9b72.

15. Mercatus Center, George Mason University. *DeSmog*. https://www.desmog.com/mercatus-center.

16. Bob Davis, July 16, 2004. "In Washington, tiny think tank wields big stick on regulation." *The Wall Street Journal*. https://www.wsj.com/articles/SB108994396555065646.

17. James A. Dorn, November 9, 2004. "Creating an ownership society: the Bush challenge." Cato Institute. https://www.cato.org/commentary/creating-ownership-society-bush-challenge.

18. Edward H. Crane, November/December 2004. "Toward the ownership society." Cato Institute (President's Message). https://www.cato.org/sites/cato.org/files/serials/files/policy-report/2004/11/cpr-26n6-2.pdf.

19. Dorn, "Creating an ownership society."

20. Crane, "Toward the ownership society."

21. Lily Geismer, December 26, 2022/January 2, 2023. "How the third way made neoliberal politics seem inevitable." *The Nation*. https://www.thenation.com/article/politics/third-way-dlc-bill-clinton-tony-blair-1990s-politics.

22. Justin H. Vassallo, July 1, 2022. "How the Democrats traded the new deal for neoliberalism." *Jacobin*. https://jacobin.com/2022/07/democratic-party-neoliberalism-dlc-clinton.

23. Robert Dreyfuss, December 19, 2001. "How the DLC does it." *The American Prospect*. https://prospect.org/features/dlc.

24. Ibid.

25. Lily Geismer, June 11, 2019. "Democrats and neoliberalism." *Vox*. https://www.vox.com/polyarchy/2019/6/11/18660240/democrats-neoliberalism.

26. Ibid.

27. Bruce Reed. Aspen Institute. https://www.aspeninstitute.org/people/bruce-reed.

28. Victor Tan Chen, January 16, 2016. "All hollowed out: the lonely poverty of America's white working class." *The Atlantic*. https://www.theatlantic.com/business/archive/2016/01/white-working-class-poverty/424341.

29. Katie Lobosco, July 1, 2020. "NAFTA is officially gone: here's

what has and hasn't changed." *CNN Politics*. https://edition.cnn
.com/2020/07/01/politics/usmca-nafta-replacement-trump
/index.html.

30. George Monbiot, November 30, 2016. "Frightened by Donald
Trump? You don't know the half of it." *The Guardian*. https://
www.theguardian.com/commentisfree/2016/nov/30/donald
-trump-george-monbiot-misinformation.

31. Alexander Bolton, January 19, 2017. "Trump team prepares dra-
matic cuts." *The Hill*. https://thehill.com/policy/finance/314991
-trump-team-prepares-dramatic-cuts.

32. The Heritage Foundation, November 1, 2016. "Blueprint for a
new administration: priorities for the president." https://www
.heritage.org/conservatism/report/blueprint-new-administration
-priorities-the-president.

33. Tamara Keith, January 20, 2021. "Trump revokes administration
ethics rules on his way out the door." National Public Radio.
https://www.npr.org/sections/inauguration-day-live-updates
/2021/01/20/958710562/trump-revokes-administration-ethics
-rules-on-his-way-out-the-door.

CHAPTER 12

ANOMIE IN THE UK

1. From *The Times*, October 13, 2006. "Obituary: Arthur Seldon
(1916–2005)." Quoted by Margaret Thatcher Foundation.
https://www.margaretthatcher.org/document/110889.

2. Adam Curtis, September 13, 2011. "The curse of Tina." BBC.
https://www.bbc.co.uk/blogs/adamcurtis/entries/fdb484c8
-99a1-32a3-83be-20108374b985.

3. Ibid.

4. Susan George, March 24, 1999. "A short history of neoliberalism."
TNI (Transnational Institute). https://www.tni.org/en/article/a
-short-history-of-neoliberalism.

5. Alejandro Chafuen, November 27, 2013. "The Fisher recipe for
successful think tanks." *Forbes*. https://www.forbes.com/sites
/alejandrochafuen/2013/11/27/the-fisher-recipe-for-successful
-think-tanks-2/?sh=4deea5846563.

6. Atlas Network. https://www.atlasnetwork.org/partners.

7. The Institute of Economic Affairs Limited. "Activities—how the

charity spends its money: data for financial year ending 31 March 2022." Charity Commission for England and Wales. https://register-of-charities.charitycommission.gov.uk/charity-details/?regid=235351&subid=0.

8. Madsen Pirie, 2012. *Think Tank: The Story of the Adam Smith Institute*. BiteBack, London.

9. "Who funds you? UK think tanks and campaigns rated for funding transparency." *open Democracy*. https://www.opendemocracy.net/en/who-funds-you.

10. *No Turning Back*, 1985. https://198047250ac5ba4d3d17-3f1b7070c0761ad2dcac8b7012ff4945.ssl.cf2.rackcdn.com/851103%20CPC%20pamphlet%20NO%20TURNING%20BACK%20THCR%202-1-4-40%20f25.pdf.

11. Who Funds You? https://www.opendemocracy.net/en/who-funds-you.

12. Jeff Judson, April 12, 2010. "21 Reasons why free-market think tanks are more effective than anyone else in changing public policy (and one reason why they are not)." https://www.scribd.com/document/30730535/Why-Think-Tanks-are-More-Effective.

13. Jane Mayer, August 23, 2010. "Covert operations." *The New Yorker*.

14. Ivana Katsarova, March 3, 2023. "World obesity day reveals a worrying picture." Think Tank, European Parliament. https://www.europarl.europa.eu/thinktank/en/document/EPRS_ATA(2023)739361#.

15. *Maid in London*, August 26, 2015. "By Giovannino again . . . so who owns this place?" http://maidinlondonnow.blogspot.com/2015_08_01_archive.html.

16. Andy Wightman, November 19, 2015. "Offshore landownership frustrates police investigation." *Land Matters*. http://www.andywightman.com/archives/4377.

17. Phillip W. Magness, December 10, 2018. "The pejorative origins of the term 'neoliberalism.'" American Institute for Economic Research. https://www.aier.org/article/the-pejorative-origins-of-the-term-neoliberalism.

18. Jonathan Chait, July 16, 2017. "How 'neoliberalism' became the left's favorite insult of liberals." Intelligencer, *New York Magazine*. https://nymag.com/intelligencer/2017/07/how-neoliberalism-became-the-lefts-favorite-insult.html.

19. Franklin D. Roosevelt, April 29, 1938. Message to Congress on Curbing Monopolies. The American Presidency Project, University of California, Santa Barbara. https://www.presidency.ucsb .edu/documents/message-congress-curbing-monopolies.

CHAPTER 13
LYING THROUGH THEIR TEETH

1. Kristian Niemietz, November 2, 2016. "Motion: 'This House would privatize the NHS.'" IEA (Institute of Economic Affairs). https://iea.org.uk/motion-this-house-would-abolish-the-nhs.

2. John Lister and Jacky Davis, 2022. *NHS Under Siege: The Fight to Save It in the Age of Covid.* The Merlin Press.

3. The King's Fund, September 20, 2023. "The NHS budget and how it has changed." https://www.kingsfund.org.uk/projects/nhs -in-a-nutshell/nhs-budget.

4. Lister and Davis, *NHS Under Siege.*

5. Toby Helm et al., January 8, 2023. "Sick man of Europe: why the crisis-ridden NHS is falling apart." *The Observer.* https://www .theguardian.com/society/2023/jan/08/sick-man-of-europe-why -the-crisis-ridden-nhs-is-falling-apart.

6. Ruth Green, Harriet Agerholm, and Libby Rogers, August 8, 2022. "Full extent of NHS dentistry shortage revealed by far-reaching BBC research." BBC. https://www.bbc.co.uk/news /health-62253893.

7. Healthwatch Suffolk, April 12, 2021. "Why you probably can't find a local NHS dentist—a system in crisis?" https:// healthwatchsuffolk.co.uk/news/dentalcrisis.

8. Anonymous dentist, February 2, 2022. "NHS dentistry: I don't want to leave, but I feel there is no choice." British Dental Association. https://bda.org/news-center/blog/Pages/NHS-dentistry-I-don %E2%80%99t-want-to-leave-but-I-feel-there-is-no-choice.aspx.

9. British Dental Association, July 22, 2022. "NHS dentists demand lifeline as 'dental inflation' soars." https://bda.org/news -center/latest-news-articles/Pages/NHS-Dentists-demand -lifeline-as-dental-inflation-soars.aspx.

10. National Audit Office, February 2020. "Dentistry in England: A National Audit Office memorandum to support a Health and

Social Care Committee inquiry." https://www.nao.org.uk/reports /dentistry-in-england.

11.   Francisco Garcia, May 30, 2022. "Superglue and self-extraction: Britain's desperate 'DIY dentistry' is a painful reality." *The Guardian.* https://www.theguardian.com/commentisfree/2022/may/30 /superglue-self-extraction-diy-dentistry-britain-nhs-dental -treatment.

12.   Shawn Charlwood, August 10, 2022. "NHS dentistry: have we reached the point of no return?" British Dental Association. https://bda.org/news-center/blog/Pages/NHS-dentistry-have -we-reached-the-point-of-no-return.aspx.

13.   Iris J. Lav and Michael Leachman, June 13, 2017. "The Trump budget's massive cuts to state and local services and programs." Center on Budget and Policy Priorities. https://www.cbpp.org /research/state-budget-and-tax/the-trump-budgets-massive -cuts-to-state-and-local-services-and.

14.   Garrett Watson, October 18, 2023. "A lower corporate rate is an opportunity worth taking as part of broader tax reform." Tax Foundation, Washington, DC. https://taxfoundation.org/blog /trump-corporate-tax-cut.

15.   Cayli Baker, December 15, 2020. "The Trump administration's major environmental deregulations." Brookings Institution. https://www.brookings.edu/articles/the-trump-administrations -major-environmental-deregulations.

16.   Lawrence J. Korb, February 28, 2018. "Trump's defense budget." Center for American Progress (CAP 20). https://www .americanprogress.org/article/trumps-defense-budget.

17.   Ibid.

CHAPTER 14
WHEN NEOLIBERALS GET EVERYTHING THEY WANT: A CASE STUDY

1.   Liz Truss et al., 2012. *Britannia Unchained.* Palgrave Macmillan, London.

2.   Matt Honeycombe-Foster, September 8, 2022. "London influence: IEA way or the highway—SpAd advice—give (time) generously." *Politico.* https://www.politico.eu/newsletter/politico

-london-influence/iea-way-or-the-highway-spad-advice-give -time-generously-2.

3. Tobacco Tactics, September 29, 2022. Free Enterprise Group. https://tobaccotactics.org/article/free-enterprise-group.

4. Adam Ramsay and Peter Geoghegan, July 10, 2018. "Dominic Raab: is he the IEA's man in government?" *openDemocracy*. https://www.opendemocracy.net/en/opendemocracyuk/dominic -raab-is-he-iea-s-man-in-government.

5. Free Market Forum. https://www.freemarketforum.org.

6. Liz Truss, August 5, 2022. Facebook. https://www.facebook.com /LizTrussMP/posts/pfbid02nRVHyDR2fVDuyLJaVyeTN pkriVP92TLgRwcjX2KsfnuRqZ2T4h637Dj5eouhZad7l.

7. Denis Campbell and Pippa Crerar, September 14, 2022. "Plans to scrap England's anti-obesity measures 'a national scandal.'" *The Guardian*. https://www.theguardian.com/society/2022/sep/14/uks -plans-to-scrap-anti-obesity-measures-national-scandal-say -campaigners.

8. Damian Carrington, September 29, 2022. "'Brexit freedoms bill' could abolish all pesticide protections, campaigners say." *The Guardian*. https://www.theguardian.com/environment/2022/sep /29/brexit-freedoms-bill-pesticide-protections.

9. Joe Mayes, July 24, 2022. "Truss promises low-tax UK invest-ment zones in pitch to Tory base." *Bloomberg*. https://www .bloomberg.com/news/articles/2022-07-24/truss-promises-low -tax-uk-investment-zones-in-pitch-to-tory-base.

10. Oliver Feeley-Sprague, April 26, 2023. "The Public Order Bill: explained." Amnesty International UK. https://www.amnesty.org .uk/blogs/campaigns-blog/public-order-bill-explained.

11. Ruth Porter, March 6, 2012. "Ruth Porter: Close DCMS, freeze benefits and pensions, scrap the regional growth fund . . . how to save up to £35 billion." *Conservative Home*. https://conservativehome .com/2012/03/06/ruth-porter-is-communications-director-at -theinstitute-of-economic-affairs-the-very-language-of-cuts -has-been-markedly-auste.

12. Rob Evans, David Pegg, and Felicity Lawrence, November 20, 2018. "Taxpayers' Alliance received over £223k in foreign dona-tions." *The Guardian*. https://www.theguardian.com/politics/2018 /nov/20/taxpayers-alliance-received-hundreds-of-thousands-in -foreign-donations.

13. Anita Mureithi, September 8, 2022. "Revealed: Truss's new economic adviser said climate change might 'balance out.'" *open-Democracy*. https://www.opendemocracy.net/en/matthew-sinclair -liz-truss-climate-change,

14. Mark Littlewood, September 23, 2022. X formerly known as Twitter. https://twitter.com/MarkJLittlewood/status/157324076 0572542976.

15. Matthew Lesh, September 23, 2022. X formerly known as Twitter. https://twitter.com/matthewlesh/status/1573219352622637056.

16. George Monbiot, October 14, 2022. X formerly known as Twitter. https://twitter.com/GeorgeMonbiot/status/158093272981 3991425.

17. Torsten Bell, November 15, 2022. "One statement, two challenges: how the Autumn Statement is likely to respond to weaker public finances and high energy bills." Resolution Foundation. https://www.resolutionfoundation.org/publications/one -statement-two-challenges.

18. Tristan Fiedler, October 18, 2022. "Liz Truss now the least-popular UK prime minister in the history of polling." *Politico*. https://www.independent.co.uk/news/uk/politics/liz-truss-poll -labour-conservatives-b2202716.html.

19. Andrew Woodcock, October 14, 2022. "Liz Truss's Tories slump below 20% in bombshell poll." *The Independent*. https://www .independent.co.uk.

CHAPTER 15
ATTACK OF THE KILLER CLOWNS

1. Thomas Piketty, 2014. *Capital in the Twenty-First Century*. Harvard University Press, Cambridge, MA.

2. Philip Rucker and Robert Costa, February 23, 2017. "Bannon vows a daily fight for 'deconstruction of the administrative state.'" *The Washington Post*. https://www.washingtonpost.com/politics /top-wh-strategist-vows-a-daily-fight-for-deconstruction-of -the-administrative-state/2017/02/23/03f6b8da-f9ea-11e6-bf01 -d47f8cf9b643_story.html.

3. Peter Thiel, April 13, 2009. "The education of a Libertarian." Cato Unbound. https://www.cato-unbound.org/2009/04/13/peter -thiel/education-libertarian.

4. Mike Lee, October 8, 2020. X formerly known as Twitter. https:// twitter.com/SenMikeLee/status/1314089207875371008.

5. Patrick Collinson, February 1, 2020. "Millions for charity . . . and Brexit: inside Peter Hargreaveses' world." *The Guardian*. https:// www.theguardian.com/business/2020/feb/01/peter-hargreaves -millions-for-charity-and-brexit-hargreaves-lansdown.

6. Staff and agencies in London, May 12, 2016. "'Like Dunkirk': Brexit donor trumpets 'fantastic insecurity' of leaving EU." *The Guardian*. https://www.theguardian.com/politics/2016/may/12 /billionaire-brexit-donor-leaving-eu-like-dunkirk.

7. Letters to the Editor, June 22, 2016. "British business 'benefits massively from EU.'" *The Times*. https://www.thetimes.co.uk /article/british-business-benefits-massively-from-eu-n5bhfw9nd.

8. June 26, 2018. "Boris Johnson challenged over Brexit business 'expletive.'" *BBC News*. https://www.bbc.co.uk/news/uk-politics -44618154.

9. Carole Cadwalladr, February 26, 2017. "Robert Mercer: the big data billionaire waging war on mainstream media." *The Guardian*. https://www.theguardian.com/politics/2017/feb/26/robert -mercer-breitbart-war-on-media-steve-bannon-donald-trump -nigel-farage.

10. The Electoral Commission: search the registers of political parties, non-party campaigners & referendum participants, and database of donations, loans, election/referendum spending & party accounts. https://search.electoralcommission.org.uk.

11. Dominic Kennedy and Oliver Wright, November 27, 2019. "Christopher Harborne: Brexit Party's bankroller has a Thai doppelgänger." *The Times*. https://www.thetimes.co.uk/article /christopher-harborne-brexit-partys-bankroller-has-a-thai -doppelgaenger-jnd0v9qdp.

12. Eleanor Langford, May 11, 2019. "Former Conservative backer Jeremy Hosking named as £200,000 donor to Nigel Farage's Brexit Party." *PoliticsHome*. https://www.politicshome.com/news /article/former-conservative-backer-jeremy-hosking-named-as -200000-donor-to-nigel-farages-brexit-party.

CHAPTER 16
CONSPIRACY FICTIONS

1. Naomi Klein, 2023. *Doppelganger: A Trip into the Mirror World*. Farrar, Straus and Giroux, New York.

2. Jules Evans, September 4, 2020. "Nazi hippies: when the New Age and Far Right overlap." *Medium*. https://gen.medium.com /nazi-hippies-when-the-new-age-and-far-right-overlap -d1a6ddcd7be4.

3. Simon Schama, 2004. *Landscape and Memory*. HarperPerennial, New York.

4. Jonathan Jarry, May 22, 2020. "The anti-vaccine movement in 2020." McGill Office for Science and Society. https://www .mcgill.ca/oss/article/covid-19-pseudoscience/anti-vaccine -movement-2020.

5. Benjy Sarlin, January 10, 2017. "Anti-vaccine activist says Trump asked him to head commission on vaccine safety." *NBC News*. https://www.nbcnews.com/politics/politics-news/trump-meets -anti-vaccine-activist-after-raising-fringe-theory-trail-n705296.

6. Derek Beres, Matthew Remski, and Julian Walker, 2023. *Conspirituality: How New Age Conspiracy Theories Became a Health Threat*. Hachette UK, London.

7. February 19, 2009, updated August 5, 2010. "Rick Santelli's shout heard 'round the world.'" *CNBC Business News*. https:// www.cnbc.com/id/29283701.

8. Alexander Hertel-Fernandez, Caroline Tervo, and Theda Skocpol, September 26, 2018. "How the Koch brothers built the most powerful right-wing group you've never heard of." *The Guardian*. https://www.theguardian.com/us-news/2018/sep/26 /koch-brothers-americans-for-prosperity-rightwing-political -group.

9. Andrew Goldman, July 23, 2010. "The billionaire's party." *New York Magazine*. https://nymag.com/news/features/67285.

10. *(Astro) Turf Wars*, 2010. "Director: Taki Oldham." *IMDb*. https:// www.imdb.com/title/tt1899098.

11. Vanessa Williamson, Theda Skocpol, and John Coggin, 2011. "The Tea Party and the remaking of Republican conservatism." *Perspectives on Politics*, vol. 9, no. 1, pp. 25–43. https://scholar .harvard.edu/files/williamson/files/tea_party_pop.pdf.

12. Jane Mayer, August 23, 2010. "Covert operations." *The New Yorker*.

13. Sean Illing, February 6, 2020. "'Flood the zone with shit': how misinformation overwhelmed our democracy." *Vox*. https://www .vox.com/policy-and-politics/2020/1/16/20991816/impeachment -trial-trump-bannon-misinformation.

14. Cassie Miller, June 1, 2022. "SPLC poll finds substantial support for 'great replacement' theory and other hard-right ideas." Southern Poverty Law Center (SPLC). https://www.splcenter.org /news/2022/06/01/poll-finds-support-great-replacement-hard -right-ideas.

15. Jared Sharpe, October 25, 2022. "New national UMASS Amherst poll on issues finds one-third of Americans believe 'great replacement' theory." University of Massachusetts, Amherst. https://www.umass.edu/news/article/new-national-umass -amherst-poll-issues-finds-one-third-americans-believe-great.

16. Mallory Newall, December 30, 2020. "More than 1 in 3 Americans believe a 'deep state' is working to undermine Trump." Ipsos. https://www.ipsos.com/en-us/news-polls/npr-misinformation -123020.

17. George Monbiot, October 3, 2019. "Demagogues thrive by whipping up our fury: here's how to thwart them." *The Guardian*. https://www.theguardian.com/commentisfree/2019/oct/03 /demagogues-fury-violence-outrage-discourse.

18. Anat Bardi and Robin Goodwin, 2011. "The dual route to value change: individual processes and cultural moderators." *Journal of Cross-Cultural Psychology*, vol. 42, no. 2. https://journals.sagepub .com/doi/10.1177/0022022110396916.

19. Peter Walker, April 8, 2019. "UK poised to embrace authoritarianism, warns Hansard Society." *The Guardian*. https://www .theguardian.com/politics/2019/apr/08/uk-more-willing-embrace -authoritarianism-warn-hansard-audit-political-engagement.

20. Matthew C. MacWilliams, September 23, 2020. "Trump is an authoritarian: so are millions of Americans." *Politico*. https:// www.politico.com/news/magazine/2020/09/23/trump-america -authoritarianism-420681.

21. Tom Hogan, January 6, 2022. "New poll: one year after Jan. 6th, disturbing support for authoritarianism." *The Bulwark*. https:// www.thebulwark.com/new-poll-one-year-after-jan-6th -disturbing-support-for-authoritarianism.

CHAPTER 17
CITIZENS OF NOWHERE

1. Adam Ramsay, December 3, 2018. "Dark money investigations: what we've found out, and why we're looking." *openDemocracy*. https://www.opendemocracy.net/en/dark-money-investigations /dark-money-investigations-what-we-ve-found-out-and-why -we-re-looking.

2. Carole Cadwalladr, May 7, 2017. "The great British Brexit robbery: how our democracy was hijacked." *The Observer*. https:// www.theguardian.com/technology/2017/may/07/the-great -british-brexit-robbery-hijacked-democracy.

3. Reijer Hendrikse and Rodrigo Fernandez, January 16, 2019. "Offshore finance: how capital rules the world." TNI (Transnational Institute). https://longreads.tni.org/stateofpower/offshore -finance.

4. Theresa May, October 5, 2016. "Theresa May's conference speech in full." *Daily Telegraph*. https://www.telegraph.co.uk/news/2016 /10/05/theresa-mays-conference-speech-in-full.

5. Salon and Conor Lynch, March 16, 2015. "Welcome to 'Libertarian Island': inside the frightening economic dreams of Silicon Valley's super rich." *AlterNet*. https://www.alternet.org/2015/03 /welcome-libertarian-island-inside-frightening-economic -dreams-silicon-valleys.

6. Rachel Riederer, May 29, 2017. "Libertarians seek a home on the high seas: the unlikely rise—and anti-democratic impulses—of seasteading." *The New Republic (TNR)*. https://newrepublic.com /article/142381/libertarians-seek-home-high-seas.

7. Ayn Rand, 1957. *Atlas Shrugged*. Random House, New York.

8. Ayn Rand, 1943. *The Fountainhead*. Bobbs Merrill, Indianapolis.

9. National Space Society (NSS). "Space settlements: spreading life throughout the solar system." https://space.nss.org/settlement /nasa.

CHAPTER 18
A FLAW IN THE MODEL

1. Tim G. Benton et al., 2017. "Environmental tipping points and food system dynamics: main report." The Global Food Security

program, UK. https://dspace.stir.ac.uk/bitstream/1893/24796/1/GFS_Tipping%20Points_Main%20Report.pdf.

2. Oleg Komlik, September 9, 2022. "Queen Elizabeth, economists and the financial crisis." *Economic Sociology & Political Economy.* https://economicsociology.org/2022/09/09/queen-elizabeth-ii-economists-and-the-financial-crisis.

3. Andrew G. Haldane and Robert M. May, 2011. "Systemic risk in banking ecosystems." *Nature*, vol. 469, pp. 351–55. https://www.nature.com/articles/nature09659.

4. Andrew G. Haldane, April 28, 2009. "Rethinking the financial network—speech by Andy Haldane." Bank of England. https://www.bankofengland.co.uk/speech/2009/rethinking-the-financial-network.

5. Adam Smith, 1759. *The Theory of Moral Sentiments.* Printed for Andrew Millar, London; and Alexander Kincaid and J. Bell, Edinburgh.

6. Maria Bustillos, April 12, 2011. "When Alan met Ayn: 'Atlas Shrugged' and our tanked economy." *The Awl.* https://www.theawl.com/2011/04/when-alan-met-ayn-atlas-shrugged-and-our-tanked-economy.

7. Associated Press, October 2, 2008. "Greenspan admits 'mistake' that helped crisis." *NBC News.* https://www.nbcnews.com/id/wbna27335454?ex=digest.

CHAPTER 19
NO EXIT

1. Friedrich Hayek, 1960. *The Constitution of Liberty.* University of Chicago Press, Chicago.

2. Our World in Data, 2020. "Calorie supply by food group, 2020." https://ourworldindata.org/grapher/calorie-supply-by-food-group?country=GBR~CHN~SWE~USA~BRA~IND~BGD.

3. Martina Sartori et al., 2019. "A linkage between the biophysical and the economic: assessing the global market impacts of soil erosion." *Land Use Policy*, vol. 86, pp. 299–312. https://www.sciencedirect.com/science/article/pii/S0264837718319343?via%3Dihub.

4. Luca Montanarella, Robert Scholes, and Anastasia Brainich, 2018. "The IPBES assessment report on land degradation and

restoration." IPBES (The Intergovernmental Science-Policy Platform on Biodiversity and Ecosystem Services). https:// digitallibrary.un.org/record/3794559.

5. UN Climate Change secretariat (UNFCCC secretariat). "Background note on the USD 100 billion goal in the context of UN-FCCC process, in relation to advancing on SDG indicator 13.a.1." https://unstats.un.org/sdgs/tierIII-indicators/files/13.a.1 _Background.pdf.

6. Jocelyn Timperley, 2021. "The broken $100-billion promise of climate finance—and how to fix it." *Nature*, vol. 598, pp. 400–02. https://www.nature.com/articles/d41586-021-02846-3.

7. BloombergNEF, July 20, 2021. "New report finds G-20 member countries support fossil fuels at levels untenable to achieve Paris Agreement goals." https://about.bnef.com/blog/new-report -finds-g-20-member-countries-support-fossil-fuels-at-levels -untenable-to-achieve-paris-agreement-goals.

8. Todd Miller, Nick Buxton, and Mark Akkerman, 2021. "Global climate wall: how the world's wealthiest nations prioritize borders over climate action." TNI (Transnational Institute). https:// www.tni.org/en/publication/global-climate-wall.

9. Laurie Laybourn Langton, April 20, 2021, updated September 8, 2021. "The age of consequences: the future for which left environmentalism is unprepared." *The New Statesman*. https:// www.newstatesman.com/environment/2021/04/the-age-of -consequences-the-future-for-which-left-environmentalism-is -unprepared.

10. Global Witness, February 9, 2023. "Crisis year 2022 brought $134 billion in excess profit to the West's five largest oil and gas companies." https://www.globalwitness.org/en/campaigns/fossil -gas/crisis-year-2022-brought-134-billion-in-excess-profit-to -the-wests-five-largest-oil-and-gas-companies.

11. Dan Welsby, 2021. "Unextractable fossil fuels in a 1.5°C world." *Nature*, vol. 597, pp. 230–34. https://www.nature.com/articles /s41586-021-03821-8.

12. IEA (Institute of Economic Affairs), revised May 2021. "Net zero by 2050: a roadmap for the global energy sector." https:// www.iea.org/reports/net-zero-by-2050.

13. Angela Picciariello et al., October 2022. "Navigating energy transitions: mapping the road to 1.5°C." IISD (International

Institute for Sustainable Development). https://www.iisd.org/publications/report/navigating-energy-transitions.

14. HM Treasury, November 17, 2022. "Policy paper, energy taxes factsheet, autumn statement 2022: summary of changes to oil and gas profits taxation." Gov.UK. https://www.gov.uk/government/publications/autumn-statement-2022-energy-taxes-factsheet/energy-taxes-factsheet.

15. Zoha Tunio, September 16, 2022. "In Pakistan, 33 million people have been displaced by climate-intensified floods." *Inside Climate News*. https://insideclimatenews.org/news/16092022/pakistan-flood-displacement.

16. Xiaogang He and Justin Sheffield, 2020. "Lagged compound occurrence of droughts and pluvials globally over the past seven decades." *Geophysical Research Letters*, vol. 47, no. 14. https://agupubs.onlinelibrary.wiley.com/doi/10.1029/2020GL087924.

17. David Eckstein, Vera Künzel, and Laura Schäfer, 2021. "Global climate risk index 2021: who suffers most from extreme weather events? Weather-related loss events in 2019 and 2000 to 2019." *Germanwatch*. https://www.germanwatch.org/en/19777.

18. Timothy M. Lenton et al., 2023. "Quantifying the human cost of global warming." *Nature Sustainability*, vol. 6, pp. 1,237–47. https://www.nature.com/articles/s41893-023-01132-6.

19. Michael Le Page, August 23, 2022. "Heatwave in China is the most severe ever recorded in the world." *New Scientist*. https://www.newscientist.com/article/2334921-heatwave-in-china-is-the-most-severe-ever-recorded-in-the-world.

20. Copernicus Climate Change Service, October 5, 2022. "Copernicus: Exceptional temperatures recorded for Greenland and joint 4th warmest September globally." https://climate.copernicus.eu/copernicus-exceptional-temperatures-recorded-greenland-and-joint-4th-warmest-september-globally.

21. Caitlin O'Kane, June 27, 2023. "Chicago has the worst air quality in the world due to Canadian wildfire smoke." *CBS News*. https://www.cbsnews.com/news/chicago-worst-air-quality-canadian-wildfire-smoke-june-27-2023.

22. Brendan O'Brien, June 29, 2023. "Canadian wildfire smoke spreads, 100 million Americans under air-quality alerts." Reuters. https://www.reuters.com/world/us/smoke-canadian-wildfires-settles-over-us-midwest-east-2023-06-29.

23.   Josephine Franks, July 25, 2023. "Sea temperature in Florida reaches 38C—potentially a world record." *SkyNews*. https://news.sky.com/story/sea-temperature-off-florida-reaches-38c-potentially-a-world-record-12927068.

24.   Ingrid Bechmann, October 18, 2022. "Providing water, food and shelter for people displaced on the Horn of Africa." UNHCR (United Nations High Commissioner for Refugees). https://www.unhcr.org/neu/86727-providing-water-food-and-shelter-for-people-displaced-on-the-horn-of-africa.html.

25.   Andrew Lilico, February 17, 2014. "We have failed to prevent global warming, so we must adapt to it." *Daily Telegraph*. https://www.telegraph.co.uk/finance/economics/10644867/We-have-failed-to-prevent-global-warming-so-we-must-adapt-to-it.html.

26.   James S. Murray, April 1, 2014. "Climate adaptation lobby is reckless, dangerous, and (partly) right." *Business Green*. https://www.businessgreen.com/blog-post/2337458/climate-adaptation-lobby-is-reckless-dangerous-and-partly-right.

CHAPTER 20

THE MICRO-SOLUTIONS MYTH

1.   Finis Dunaway, November 21, 2017. "The 'Crying Indian' ad that fooled the environmental movement." *Chicago Tribune*. https://www.chicagotribune.com/opinion/commentary/ct-perspec-indian-crying-environment-ads-pollution-1123-20171113-story.html.

2.   Keep Britain Tidy, 2012. "Love where you live and get involved." https://www.keepbritaintidy.org/sites/default/files/resources/KBT_Love-Where-You-Live-and-Get-Involved_2012.pdf.

3.   Tobacco Tactics, April 27, 2020. "CSR: imperial and love where you live." https://tobaccotactics.org/article/csr-imperial-and-love-where-you-live.

4.   Mark Kaufman. "The carbon footprint sham: Mashable's social good series, Mashable India." https://in.mashable.com/science/15520/the-carbon-footprint-sham.

5.   Emily Gosden, June 11, 2019. "Eat seasonally and recycle more to cut emissions, says Shell." *The Times*. https://www.thetimes

.co.uk/article/shell-asks-businesses-to-work-together-in-cutting -emissions-0pwkk2qnm.

6. Ron Bousso, Bart H. Meijer, and Shadia Nasralla, May 26, 2021. "Shell ordered to deepen carbon cuts in landmark Dutch climate case." Reuters. https://www.reuters.com/business/sustainable -business/dutch-court-orders-shell-set-tougher-climate-targets -2021-05-26.

7. Stanley Reed, June 9, 2021. "Shell says a court ruling on green-house gases will speed up its plans to cut emissions." *The New York Times*. https://www.nytimes.com/2021/06/09/business/shell -climate-change.html.

8. Zoë Schlanger, April 1, 2019. "Your cotton tote is pretty much the worst replacement for a plastic bag." *Quartz*. https://qz .com/1585027/when-it-comes-to-climate-change-cotton-totes -might-be-worse-than-plastic.

9. Laura Sullivan, September 11, 2020. "How big oil misled the pub-lic into believing plastic would be recycled." NPR (National Public Radio). https://www.npr.org/2020/09/11/897692090/how-big-oil -misled-the-public-into-believing-plastic-would-be-recycled.

10. Ibid.

11. Ibid.

12. Andrea Tabi, 2013. "Does pro-environmental behavior affect car-bon emissions?" *Energy Policy*, vol. 63, pp. 972–81. https://www .sciencedirect.com/science/article/abs/pii/S0301421513008537.

13. Jonas Nässén, September 26, 2014. "Explaining the variation in greenhouse gas emissions between households: socioeconomic, motivational, and physical factors." *Journal of Industrial Ecology*, vol. 19, no. 3, pp. 480–89. https://www.researchgate.net/publication /266206723_Explaining_the_Variation_in_Greenhouse_Gas _Emissions_Between_Households_Socioeconomic_Motivational _and_Physical_Factors.

14. Michael J. Lynch et al., 2019. "Measuring the ecological im-pact of the wealthy: excessive consumption, ecological disorga-nization, green crime, and justice." *Social Currents*, vol. 6, no. 4, pp. 377–95. https://journals.sagepub.com/doi/abs/10.1177 /2329496519847491.

15. Tim Gore, November 5, 2021. "Carbon inequality in 2030." Oxfam International. https://www.oxfam.org/en/research/carbon -inequality-2030.

16. Tim Gore, 2021. "Carbon inequality in 2030: per capita consumption emissions and the 1.5°C goal." Oxfam Policy & Practice. https://policy-practice.oxfam.org/resources/carbon-inequality -in-2030-per-capita-consumption-emissions-and-the-15c-goal -621305.

17. Richard Wilk and Beatriz Barros, February 16, 2021. "Private planes, mansions and superyachts: what gives billionaires like Musk and Abramovich such a massive carbon footprint." *The Conversation.* https://theconversation.com/private-planes-mansions -and-superyachts-what-gives-billionaires-like-musk-and-abram ovich-such-a-massive-carbon-footprint-152514.

18. Giacomo Tognini, January 6, 2023. "Russian billionaire Roman Abramovich owns 16 yachts and vessels, 10 more than previously known." *Forbes.* https://www.forbes.com/sites/giacomotognini /2023/01/06/russian-billionaire-roman-abramovich-owns-16 -yachts-and-vessels-10-more-than-previously-known.

19. George Monbiot, March 14, 2014. "How a false solution to climate change is damaging the natural world." *The Guardian.* https://www.theguardian.com/environment/georgemonbiot /2014/mar/14/uk-ban-maize-biogas.

CHAPTER 21
MOBILIZATION: A CASE STUDY

1. Dean C. Allard, June 25, 1991. "Gearing up for victory: American military and industrial mobilization in World War II." *Naval History and Heritage Command*, Colloquium on Contemporary History, no. 5. https://www.history.navy.mil/research/library /online-reading-room/title-list-alphabetically/g/gearing-up -victory.html.

2. Jeff Haden, December 7, 2011. "How would you feel about a 94% tax rate?" *CBS News*, MoneyWatch. https://www.cbsnews.com /news/how-would-you-feel-about-a-94-tax-rate.

3. Historical Tables, Office of Management and Budget, President's Budget. The White House. https://www.whitehouse.gov/omb /budget/historical-tables.

4. "The auto industry goes to war." Teachinghistory.org. https:// teachinghistory.org/history-content/ask-a-historian/24088.

5. A. J. Baime, March 19, 2020. "How Detroit factories retooled dur-

ing WWII to defeat Hitler." History.com. https://www.history
.com/news/wwii-detroit-auto-factories-retooled-homefront.

6. "Take a closer look: America goes to war." National WWII
Museum New Orleans. https://www.nationalww2museum.org
/students-teachers/student-resources/research-starters/america
-goes-war-take-closer-look.

7. Allard, "Gearing up for victory."

8. "Research starters: US military by the numbers." National WWII
Museum New Orleans. https://www.nationalww2museum.org
/students-teachers/student-resources/research-starters/research
-starters-us-military-numbers.

9. Katelyn Fatzler, January 23, 1942. "Government bans U.S. auto
production." *World War 2.0.* https://blogs.shu.edu/ww2-0/1942
/01/23/government-bans-u-s-auto-production.

10. "When you ride alone, you ride with Hitler!" National Archives
(USA), Powers of Persuasion. https://www.archives.gov/exhibits
/powers_of_persuasion/use_it_up/images_html/ride_with
_hitler.html.

11. Weston D. Eastman. *The homefront during WWII.* http://
wdeastman.com/the-homefront-during-wwii.

12. The Consumer's Victory Pledge. Student Handouts. https://
www.studenthandouts.com/american-history/11-new-deal
-world-war-ii/pictures/consumers-victory-pledge-wwii-poster
.htm.

CHAPTER 22
A NEW STORY

1. Keith Jensen, Amrisha Vaish, and Marco F. H. Schmidt, 2014.
"The emergence of human prosociality: aligning with others
through feelings, concerns, and norms." *Frontiers in Psychology*,
vol. 5, p. 822. https://www.frontiersin.org/articles/10.3389/fpsyg
.2014.00822/full.

2. Common Cause Foundation, 2016. "Perceptions matter: the
Common Cause UK values survey." Common Cause Foundation, London. https://commoncausefoundation.org/_resources
/perceptions-matter-report-summary.

CHAPTER 23
THE POLITICS OF BELONGING

1. Murray Bookchin, 2015. *The Next Revolution: Popular Assemblies and the Promise of Direct Democracy*. Verso, New York.

2. Cihad Hammy and Thomas Jeffrey Miley, 2022. "Lessons from Rojava for the paradigm of social ecology." *Frontiers in Political Science*, vol. 3, 815338. https://www.frontiersin.org/articles/10.3389/fpos.2021.815338/full.

3. Sónia Gonçalves, 2014. "The effects of participatory budgeting on municipal expenditures and infant mortality in Brazil." *World Development*, vol. 53, pp. 94–110. https://www.sciencedirect.com/science/article/abs/pii/S0305750X13000156.

4. Martin Calisto Friant, 2018. "Deliberating for sustainability: lessons from the Porto Alegre experiment with participatory budgeting." *International Journal of Urban Sustainable Development*, vol. 11, no. 1, pp. 81–99. https://www.tandfonline.com/doi/full/10.1080/19463138.2019.1570219.

5. vTaiwan. https://vtaiwan.tw.

6. "Decide Madrid: Madrid City Council's citizen participation portal." Ayuntamiento de Madrid. https://decide.madrid.es.

7. Barcelona Digital City: Decidim Barcelona. Ajuntament de Barcelona. https://ajuntament.barcelona.cat/digital/en/digital-empowerment/democracy-and-digital-rights/decidim-barcelona.

8. Lisboa Participa: Portal da Participaçao. Lisbon City Council. https://lisboaparticipa.pt/pt.

9. G1000: Doing Democracy Better. Belgium. https://www.g1000.org/en.

10. City of Melbourne. Future Melbourne. https://www.melbourne.vic.gov.au/about-melbourne/future-melbourne/Pages/future-melbourne.aspx.

11. Agata Hidalgo and Mauricio Mejia, January 9, 2020. "Avoin Ministerio: the quest for an Open Ministry. Successes and drawbacks from a Finnish experiment." https://medium.com/the-hitchhikers-guide-to-digital-democracy/avoin-ministerio-the-quest-for-an-open-ministry-a2f55f9f52c3.

12. International Observatory on Participatory Democracy (IOPD). Seoul's Participatory Budgeting. https://oidp.net/en/practice.php?id=1302.

13. Alex Altman, May 13, 2015. "Meet the man who invented the super PAC." *Time*. https://time.com/3856427/super-pac-david-keating.

14. Drew Desilver and Patrick Van Kessel, December 7, 2015. "As more money flows into campaigns, Americans worry about its influence." Pew Research Center. https://www.pewresearch.org/short-reads/2015/12/07/as-more-money-flows-into-campaigns-americans-worry-about-its-influence.

CHAPTER 24
PRIVATE SUFFICIENCY, PUBLIC LUXURY

1. George Monbiot, October 2020. "Private sufficiency, public luxury: land is the key to the transformation of society." Fortieth Annual E. F. Schumacher Lectures, Schumacher Center for a New Economics. https://centerforneweconomics.org/publications/private-sufficiency-public-luxury-land-is-the-key-to-the-transformation-of-society.

2. Silke Helfrich and David Bollier, 2019. *Free, Fair and Alive: The Insurgent Power of the Commons*. New Society Publishers, Canada.

3. Ingrid Robeyns, 2019. "What, if anything, is wrong with extreme wealth?" *Journal of Human Development and Capabilities*, vol. 20, no. 3, pp. 251–66. https://www.tandfonline.com/doi/full/10.1080/19452829.2019.1633734.

CHAPTER 25
THE TIPPING POINT

1. John Snow Project Editorial, March 30, 2023. "Merchants of doubt." The John Snow Project. https://johnsnowproject.org/insights/merchants-of-doubt.

2. Ricarda Winkelmann et al., 2022. "Social tipping processes toward climate action: a conceptual framework." *Ecological Economics*, vol. 192, pp. 107–242. https://www.sciencedirect.com/science/article/abs/pii/S0921800921003013.

3. Damon Centola, June 8, 2018. "Experimental evidence for tipping points in social convention." *Science*, vol. 360, no. 6,393, pp. 1,116–19. https://www.science.org/doi/abs/10.1126/science.aas8827.

INDEX

ABOUT THE AUTHORS

GEORGE MONBIOT is an author, *Guardian* columnist, and environmental campaigner. His books include *Feral, Heat,* and *Regenesis.*

monbiot.com

PETER HUTCHISON is a filmmaker, author, educator, and activist. His films include *Requiem for the American Dream* (featuring Noam Chomsky), *Devil Put the Coal in the Ground, Healing from Hate,* and *The Cure for Hate.*